GOOD MEMORY—
SUCCESSFUL STUDENT!

Also by Harry Lorayne

The Memory Book *with Jerry Lucas*
Remembering People
Good Memory—Good Student!

GOOD MEMORY—
SUCCESSFUL
STUDENT!

A Guide to Remembering What You Learn

by Harry Lorayne

STEIN AND DAY/*Publishers*/New York

First Stein and Day paperback edition, 1976
First published in 1973
Copyright © 1973 by Harry Lorayne
Library of Congress Catalog Card No. 73-14940
All rights reserved
Printed in the United States of America
Stein and Day/*Publishers*/Scarborough House
Briarcliff Manor, N. Y. 10510
ISBN 0-8128-2008-7

For my son Robert
and his mother Renée—
the two people who most inspire me

There is memory without learning, but there is no learning without memory.

CONTENTS

1

IF YOU CAN READ...

If you can read, you can learn the systems in this book. They are basic and simple, once you have grasped the idea and have learned the fundamentals.

If you want to improve your memory, don't skim or scan this book—*read* it! Take all the tests, even if a particular subject is of no interest to you. Answer the questions, fill in the blanks, and be actively, not just passively, involved.

Sometimes I will have to use many words and give you several examples to explain really simple ideas. There is no way to avoid that; it always takes more time to put thoughts into words than it does for the thoughts themselves to form. It may take hundreds of words to explain something that takes only a split second to think.

Although the number of years that have gone by is something I'd rather forget, I can still remember the fear of not remembering what I was supposed to remember for tests or classroom work. No, I was not born with the memory I have today. More precisely, I was born with it, just as you were, but I didn't know how to use it.

I also remember frantic hours of cramming, and the knowledge that even if I did remember the answers to the questions asked on a test, they would fade away almost immediately afterward.

If you would like to remember whatever you want to, easily, if you would like to have more leisure time—time you'd ordinarily spend on cramming—and still become a better student, then this book is dedicated to you.

Don't misunderstand me. Merely memorizing something is

9

not the same as learning or knowing it. Learning is an adventure; learning is discovery—you don't want to miss that! And you would miss it if you thought only of memorizing facts.

The memory systems in this book will make your understanding and comprehension deeper, your learning capacity larger, and your enjoyment keener. The thrill and enjoyment of learning should—and will—stay with you all your life, if you start that habit now.

There is, however, no way to separate learning and memory; they are unalterably linked. In order to learn, you must be able to remember. To learn is to absorb ideas, then to apply them. Memory is the bridge between the two. The systems explained in the following pages will not only give you a terrific memory, they will also start you using your imagination, observation, and concentration—all of which are part of the joy of learning.

2

FILLING THE GAP

There are three basic learning skills: finding the information you need, remembering the information you find, and understanding and organizing that information so that you can use it properly. It is with the second skill, remembering, that this book is concerned.

The teaching of the basic skill of remembering information has been almost totally ignored by our educational system. It is a large and obvious gap. Nevertheless, men have been attempting to fill that gap since ancient times. As long ago as 500 B.C., the Greek poet Simonides was using, teaching, and writing about the art of a trained memory. He became known as the father of the art. Aristotle, Plato, Cicero, and other ancient philosophers also taught, used, and wrote about the art of memory.

In the thirteenth century, Saint Thomas Aquinas taught the art and wrote books on the subject. He is known by some scholars as the patron saint of memory. Francis Bacon wrote books about it.

It is said that Leibnitz discovered calculus while searching for a mnemonic (memory) system for numbers. Shakespeare's Globe Theater was called a memory theater, because there were things in the architecture that could act as "pegs" to help actors remember their lines.

Through the centuries, scholars have bettered, enlarged, and used systems of memory. So, you see, they are not new and I am indeed in good company.

If you read, study, and learn the methods in this book—learn the fundamentals—and then apply the methods to the information you want to remember, you'll find that the gap in our educational system has been filled.

Of course, there are those who don't (or won't) agree that a gap exists at all. They refuse to admit that memory is important—no, essential—to education. All the same, one definition given for the word "culture" is man's accumulated knowledge and experience. Education is really nothing more than the storing up of knowledge and truth, and there is no way to extract memory from that concept.

3

ABOUT MEMORY

Although many books have been written that are supposed to help the student study, for some asinine reason nobody wants to admit that studying is based largely on memory. All the methods of study that I've read have simply neglected and overlooked that one possible and necessary aid—the *art of a trained memory*.

But let's stop kidding ourselves! If you're a high school or college student, you don't have to be told that the better your memory is, the better your grades will be. If you can remember what you are studying, then, and only then, will your studying and learning be easier and less time-consuming. Memory is the stepping-stone to thinking. There can hardly be one without the other. Without memory all intelligence and learning is lost. All knowledge is based on memory.

One of the students at the Harry Lorayne School of Memory told me that he'd spoken to a study counselor at his high school about his supposedly bad memory. The counselor told him that he'd have to do the best he could. That was it; nothing could be done about it.

That was probably the worst piece of counseling ever given. Had this student not heard of me and come for help, he'd have been condemned to poor grades for the remainder of his school career. Worse than that, he would have lived the rest of his life thinking that he was born with a poor memory. As a result, he would have actually *had* a poor memory. It's like eating a bad piece of pie the first time you try pie, and living the rest of your life thinking that that is how pie tastes!

We are all born with the capacity to remember. Your memory is no worse than the next person's; it's just a matter of using it properly. Because you may be having some difficulty studying now, is no reason to condemn yourself to a poor memory forever.

You *can* better your memory! You can use the memory you have now to much better advantage. You can stimulate and use it to remember and retain whatever you like, easily and quickly.

Incidentally, I am well aware of the fact that the trend in education today is to get away from rote memory. The students are to learn by doing and by understanding concepts. Some of the teachers I interviewed would not even use the word "memory"—not until I really pinned them down, anyway.

Of course, trying to help a student learn by doing and through concepts is great. But we all still know that in order to pass any subject or to pass most tests—to learn—you'd better *remember!*

I had a similar discussion with a history teacher some time ago. His argument was that memory was unimportant in education today. Then I sat in at his beginning-of-term class. He told his students that on page so-and-so of the text was a list of all the Presidents of the United States and the dates of their terms in office. He said, "You must all know the Presidents in chronological order, and the dates, before the end of this term. If you don't learn them, you can't pass this subject."

Well, he used the words "know" and "learn"—never "remember" or "memorize"—but isn't that what he really meant? He sure did! Because there's no way to know or learn the names and the sequence of the terms of all the Presidents, and the dates, without memorizing or remembering them! No way at all.

That's just one example. Another is the teacher who had a chart listing all the chemical elements and symbols on the blackboard. When I asked her if the students had to memorize them, or if they'd be better off if they did, she said, "Oh, no. We don't believe in memory anymore. The students learn by doing and by concept."

I finally asked her whether a student wouldn't be better off, or receive a better mark on a test if he or she could fill in the blank in this question, "Fe = ... ," with the word "iron."

She said, "Of course." I asked her to tell me which mental process the student would be using in order to fill in that blank correctly. It took me fifteen minutes to get her to admit that the mental process was—memory.

Doing and concepts are fine, but without memory, they don't hold up too well. In fact, the doing-and-concept idea itself is a method that's supposed to help you remember information! The same is true of most subjects that you study. If you have a good memory, you're a good student. You think with what you remember, because memory is knowledge. What you remember, you *know*.

Even though some teachers won't admit that memory is important, I'm sure most of them are well aware of it. At least I know that that is one way they judge and grade students. They are *told* to judge and grade that way.

Recently I leafed through a booklet that is printed by the Board of Education of the City of New York. It is written as a guide for the teacher in judging the skills of students in reading—reading in any subject. Here are some examples of references to memory in that booklet:

"Much [of the student's] schoolwork . . . deals with [using] what is read. He sees relationships and organizes information into patterns useful for studying and *remembering*."

"[The student] shows ability to *retain and recall* what has been read."

"[The student] begins to develop more organized methods for *recalling information*."

"[The student] develops a *system* for *memorizing blocks of information*." The italics are mine.

That last reference is interesting. It tells the teacher to judge the student well if he's developed a system for memorizing. Wouldn't it be marvelous if you were taught such a system in school? Well, bettering your memory is only a matter of knowing how, and that is what I am going to show you.

With some exceptions, I find that all memory work in high school and college falls into three main categories: numbers; numbers in conjunction with names, words, or events; and reading material, which includes such things as vocabulary and terminology. The trained memory systems in this book can easily be applied to these categories, and to the exceptions, whatever they may be.

Using your memory is a skill and an art. As with any skill or art, it must be learned from the beginning; there are no shortcuts at first. The material you're about to delve into is probably completely new to you. It's an area of thinking that may seem silly at first, but don't make the mistake of thinking that something is silly just because you never heard of it before, or because it is foreign to you. Once you get past the fundamentals, you'll begin to realize how practical, fascinating, and nonsilly it is.

You are going to learn three separate methods, or ideas, based on the same rules and principles, with the same goals. They can be used separately or they can be combined. They are the basis of all my memory systems. Once you understand them and can apply them to your studies, you will have the beginnings of a trained memory.

However, before you learn these basic methods, it is important for you to know that the secret of a good, or fantastic, memory is Original Awareness.

Let me explain just what I mean by Original Awareness. Usually when someone says he has forgotten something, it means he never remembered it in the first place. You can't forget something you never knew. On the other hand, anything that registers in your mind is easy to remember later and hard to forget.

That's what I mean by Original Awareness—forcing something to register in your mind or memory in the first place. The systems in this book force you to be Originally Aware of any information the first time you see, hear, or read that information.

Therefore, the one rule that holds true for all memory, trained or untrained, is this: *In order to remember any new piece of information, it must be associated with something you already know or remember.* Association, pertaining to memory, simply means the tying together or connecting of two or more things.

That rule is the crux, the basis, of all memory. Association is something you've been using all your life. All memory is based on association, and anything you've ever remembered you have associated with something else. The problem is, you've always done it subconsciously, without thinking about it or realizing it. Now you must have the goal of *knowingly and consciously* associating everything you want to remember with some other thing. The Link and Peg systems of memory will enable you to do just that.

It is a fact that abstract or intangible information is much more difficult to remember than concrete, tangible, and meaningful information. The Substitute Word system of memory will solve that problem for you by making abstract information tangible and meaningful in your mind. Once you've learned this system, intangible material will be just as easy to memorize as any other material.

These, then, are the three ideas this book is concerned with: the Link, Peg, and Substitute Word systems of memory. They will serve as a natural extension of subconscious association. To make sure you learn and understand the Link and Peg systems well, we will take them up first in "stunt" form. As you learn and practice them, you may not see how they could apply to your studies, but don't worry about that. You must learn the fundamentals first, and then apply them to your studies.

Since you will be learning these ideas in stunt form, you may want to show off with them for family and friends. That's fine; there's nothing wrong with that. Besides, the more you use these methods, the better they will work for you the next time. Be sure, though, that you thoroughly understand them before showing off.

Once you learn the ideas, make it a game to see how many items you can remember by applying them. Do it for fun. It *is* fun to remember things using these systems.

4

SOME ASSOCIATIONS
YOU MAY HAVE USED

As I've mentioned, associations have helped you to remember things all your life. Unfortunately, you didn't know you were using associations, so you had no control over them.

If you studied music during your early grades, your teacher probably helped you remember the lines on the treble clef, *E, G, B, D,* and *F,* by telling you to think of the sentence, "*E*very *g*ood *b*oy *d*oes *f*ine."

Probably without realizing it, that teacher was following the rule I gave you a little while ago: He was helping you to remember something new and meaningless, *E, G, B, D,* and *F,* by associating it with something you already knew or understood, "Every good boy does fine." And it did work, didn't it? You still remember it!

Most of the rules you were given by your teachers were attempts to help you to remember. They were memory aids, like the spelling rule "*I* before *E,* except after *C.*"

When I was in an early grade, the students in my class were having trouble remembering the spelling of the word "believe." The teacher said something I've never forgotten. She said, "Remember this phrase, 'Never believe a lie.'" And she wrote be*LIE*ve on the blackboard. She was helping us to associate something we already knew, the spelling of *lie,* with something we didn't know, the spelling of *believe.* None of us in that class ever again had trouble spelling that word.

You probably can't remember the shape of Germany, Romania, France, Portugal, or Poland. But do you remember the shape of Italy? If you ever heard or noticed for yourself that Italy is shaped like a boot, then you remember the shape of Italy.

That's a good example of how association works, and of the rule I gave you. The shape of Italy, which was something new and intangible, was associated with the shape of a boot, something you already knew or remembered. And it certainly worked!

If you want to remember the names of the five Great Lakes, picture many *homes* on a lake. Homes will help you remember *H*uron, *O*ntario, *M*ichigan, *E*rie, and *S*uperior. Picture yourself about to *stab* four people who are singing, and it will help you to remember that a quartet consists of a *s*oprano, a *t*enor, an *a*lto, and a *b*ass.

Acronyms like these can come in handy every so often, and they sometimes get quite sophisticated. One high school student told me that the members of his class remembered the different forms of energy by thinking of the word "McHales." If the student is familiar with the forms of energy to begin with, "McHales" could remind him of *m*echanical, *c*hemical, *h*eat, *a*tomic, *l*ight, *e*lectrical, and *s*olar. One problem, of course, is that the student might not remember that word when he's asked about forms of energy, but that problem is easily solved by the Substitute Word system of memory, as you will see.

Many years ago, I learned that Mount Fujiyama in Japan is 12,365 feet high. I've always remembered that because I associated Mount Fujiyama with a calendar, and I pictured to myself a mountain made up of millions of calendars. Why a calendar? Because that reminded me of the *12* months and *365* days in a year. That is the height of Mount Fujiyama— 12,365 feet. The trouble is, I've yet to find anything else that is 12,365 feet high, wide, long, or deep!

You can remember the colors of the spectrum by imagining a boy rigging up, or building, a large letter *V*. The *V* is all different colors. If you know the colors in the first place, *BOY RIG V* would remind you of *b*lue, *o*range, *y*ellow, *r*ed, *i*ndigo, *g*reen, and *v*iolet.

There's another memory aid that just about everybody has used at one time or another. That is the rhyme that helps us remember the number of days in different months. "Thirty days hath September, April, June, and November. . . ."

Many people, of course, can't remember the rhyme in the first place, or they remember it incorrectly. There's an easier, and more interesting, way.

Close both of your hands into fists and place the fists side by side, backs of hands up. Starting on the knuckle of your left little finger, moving from left to right, and including the valleys, or spaces, between the knuckles, recite the twelve months. Thumbs are not counted. The months that fall *on* the knuckles are months with thirty-one days. The valleys represent the months with thirty days or fewer. The simple diagram below will make this clear. The months in parentheses show that if you can use one hand only, it will still work.

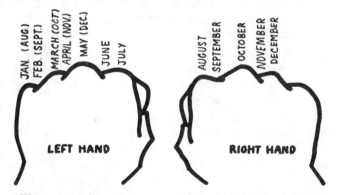

There are other ways to use these simple ideas, but the problem is that they are limited. They can be applied only to certain specific things. I want you to be able to associate (remember) *anything*. I think you'll agree, when you've finished this book, that my memory systems are unlimited and can be applied to anything—to any kind of information, at any time, and under any circumstances.

5

THE LINK SYSTEM OF MEMORY

Although you probably won't be able to see how this chapter and the next two or three can possibly apply to your studies, take my word for it—they will. You're laying a foundation, so to speak, so be sure to read and understand this chapter. The same applies to the next two or three chapters.

Let me show you first how easy it is to apply the rule I mentioned before: In order to remember any new piece of information, it must be associated, *in some ridiculous way,* with something you already know or remember. Notice the addition of the phrase *in some ridiculous way.* That is an important and necessary part of the rule for a trained memory.

Ordinarily, if I were to ask you to memorize, say, ten items in sequence after hearing or reading them only once, you'd think it impossible. And you'd be right! Ordinarily, you couldn't do it. But once you learn to apply the above rule, you'll see how easy it is. That's what the Link system of memory is all about. Its purpose is to help you remember any number of things in sequence.

Here are ten items we can use as examples: lamp, paper, bottle, bed, fish, telephone, window, flower, nail, typewriter. To apply the rule, we're going to make ridiculous mental pictures or associations between two items at a time, until we've associated, or Linked, all ten of them. Don't let this frighten you. It's easy—and it's fun!

The first thing you must do is to get a picture of the first item, *lamp,* in your mind. You know what a lamp is, so just "see" a lamp in your mind's eye. If you have a special, or favorite, lamp at home, picture that one. At first something familiar will be easier to picture; after that, it won't matter.

We can start applying the rule now if we make a couple of assumptions. We'll assume that lamp is the thing you already remember, and also that the new thing, the thing you want to remember, is *paper*. All right. Let's associate lamp with paper. That is, let's form a ridiculous picture involving both of them. The picture *must* be ridiculous—or impossible. Make it as crazy or as silly as you like.

For example, you might see a picture in your mind of a gigantic piece of paper with a string attached. You pull the string and the paper lights up like a lamp!

Or you might see yourself writing on a lamp instead of on a piece of paper. Or a lamp is writing on a piece of paper. Or a gigantic piece of paper is lighting a lamp. Do you see what I mean?

There are many ways to form a ridiculous association between any two items. Don't ever use a logical picture. An example of a logical picture, the kind not to use, might be that of a piece of paper lying next to, or near, a lamp. That's too logical; it's possible—and *it will not work*.

The second step is to see clearly in your mind for a split second or so the picture you've selected, or thought of yourself. Imagine that it's actually happening. Really see that picture. Why don't you stop reading now for a few seconds and see the ridiculous picture you've selected of a lamp and paper? Do it now.

Did you try to see the ridiculous picture of a lamp and paper? I hope so. The only way you'll see whether or not this system works is by trying it. And I'll tell you something else; even if the system didn't work, just trying to apply it must better your memory.

From now on, whenever I tell you to "see the picture," stop reading and *really see it* in your mind's eye.

Okay. If you've seen that picture, stop thinking about it now. "Forget" it, and let's continue. The next item is *bottle*.

Now you have to make a ridiculous association between paper and bottle. Don't try to think about lamp at all now.

For paper and bottle, you might see paper pouring out of a bottle instead of liquid. Or a gigantic bottle made of paper. Or you're writing on a large sheet of paper with a bottle. Or a large sheet of paper is drinking from a bottle. Select one or use one you've thought of yourself (as long as it's ridiculous or impossible) and, most important, *see that picture* in your mind for a second. Do it now.

The next item is *bed*. So now you have to associate bottle with bed. Try to think of your own ridiculous pictures. Since this is an individual and personal thing, you'll be better off if you do. What I think is ridiculous may not seem ridiculous to you, and vice versa. But more important, when you think up your own ridiculous picture, you are concentrating on those two items, or pieces of information, as you never have before!

I'll keep giving you suggestions all the way through, however, since this is the first time you've tried this idea. For bottle and bed, you might see yourself sleeping in a gigantic bottle instead of a bed. Or you're drinking from a bed instead of a bottle. Or a large bottle is sleeping in a bed. Or millions of bottles are piled on your bed. Select one of these ridiculous pictures and see it in your mind's eye.

The next item is *fish*. You can use the same ideas. See a large fish sleeping in a bed, getting it all wet. Or you're sleeping on a gigantic fish instead of a bed. Or you're fishing and you catch a bed! See in your mind for a second whichever one you think is most ridiculous.

I realize, incidentally, that when you try this for the first time, you may find it a bit strange forming ridiculous pictures. We've been brought up to think logically, and I'm telling you to think illogically. That's all right. If you have to make a slight effort, that's good. That effort will help you at first.

There are, by the way, four simple ideas that can help make your pictures ridiculous or impossible. One way is to see an item larger than life—that is, Out of Proportion. That's why I've used the word "gigantic" in some examples—to force you to do just that.

Another way is to Exaggerate the number of items. You might have pictured yourself lighting a lamp and a million pieces of paper flying out of it.

Try to get Action or Violence into your picture. Unfortunately, violence is easy to remember. If you pictured the million pieces of paper flying out of the lamp and hitting you in the face, that would be Action or Violence.

Finally, you can use the rule of Substitution—that is, simply picture one item instead of the other. If you pictured yourself catching a bed instead of a fish, that's Substitution. Or you could have pictured yourself sleeping on a gigantic fish instead of a bed. If you pictured yourself getting all wet as you slept on the fish, that would be Action.

So you see that you can get one or more of these ideas into your pictures to help make them ridiculous. After a short while, you'll do it automatically.

All right. The last item we remembered was fish. The new item is *telephone*. Form a ridiculous association in your mind between those two items. You might see a gigantic fish talking on the telephone and dripping all over the rug. Or you're talking into a fish instead of a telephone. Or you're talking on the phone and a million fish fly out of it and hit you. Or a large telephone is fishing. Select one and, most important, see the picture.

The next item is *window*. Form a ridiculous picture between telephone and window. Perhaps you see yourself tossing a gigantic telephone through a closed window and smashing that window into a million pieces. Or you're opening a large telephone, instead of a window, to look out into the street. Or a window is making a phone call. See the picture you select.

The next item is *flower*. You might see windows growing in a garden, instead of flowers—see yourself watering them. Or you have large flowers on your walls instead of windows. Or you open your window and millions of flowers fly into your house. See the picture.

The next item is *nail*. You're hammering a large flower into the wall instead of a nail. Or gigantic nails are growing instead of flowers. Or a gigantic flower is hammering a nail into a wall. Or you're hammering a gigantic nail through a gigantic flower. Select one, or think of one yourself, and see that picture.

The last item is *typewriter*. You're hammering a gigantic nail through a new typewriter, ruining it. Or all the keys on your typewriter are nails and you prick your fingers as you type. Or you're hammering a typewriter into the wall. See the picture. Don't think that because this is the last item, you'll remember it anyway. You won't if you don't make the association.

If you haven't tried to see all the pictures in your mind, go back and do it now. If you really have tried, get ready to amaze yourself! You will most likely remember all ten of the items in sequence. Want to try it? All right. Get a pencil and fill in the blanks that follow.

I'll tell you the first item because I haven't suggested a way to handle that yet (see the Questions and Answers section at the end of the chapter). The first item is lamp. Think of lamp for a moment. What does it make you think of? You were doing something silly or crazy with the lamp. Or something else was *being* a lamp. Lamp should remind you of *paper*.

If you wrote "paper" in the blank, you're correct. Now think of paper. What does that make you think of? Paper should remind you of *bottle*

Bottle is right! Think of bottle for a moment. What does it remind you of? Bottle makes you think of *bed*.

If you wrote "bed," you're absolutely right. Now think of bed for a moment; it should remind you of *fish*.

Fish is correct. Think of fish, which should make you think of *telephone*

Yes, that's right—telephone. Telephone will make you think of *window*

If you wrote "window," you're right, and you've made good ridiculous pictures. Window will make you think of *flowers*

Flower is correct. What were you doing with that flower, or what was growing instead of flowers? Perhaps you were hammering a flower instead of *nail*.

Yes, nail is correct. And finally, nail should remind you of *typewriter*

If you wrote "typewriter," you're correct. Did you fill in all the blanks correctly? You should have—and you should be proud of yourself! You've done something that most people can't do. You've memorized ten items in sequence after reading them only once.

If you had trouble with one or two, that's all right. Just go back and strengthen that particular association—that is, make sure the picture is ridiculous enough, and see it clearly. Remember, you need to see the picture for only a second. It's not the length of time that's important, it's the clarity of the picture that does the trick.

Try it on your own now. Get a pencil and paper and see if you can list all the items from lamp to typewriter. You will see that you can do it.

Now try this: Think of typewriter. That reminds you of what? A nail, of course. Think of nail. That reminds you of ... flower. Right. Flower makes you think of ... sure, window. Think of window and you're reminded of . . . telephone. Right! Telephone should make you think of . . . fish. Fish will automatically remind you of . . . bed. Bed makes you think of . . . bottle. Bottle reminds you of . . . paper. And finally, paper reminds you of . . . lamp.

Did you work along with me? If you did, do you realize that you knew the items *backward?* If you make the pictures ridiculous and really see them in your mind, you should be able to remember items forward and backward!

I call this the Link system of memory because what you're doing is forming a chain of the items you want to remember. You can retain such a list of items for as long as you want to, or as long as you need to remember the information. All you'd have to do is go over the Link mentally every once in a while. It takes no time at all. Of course, once you've remembered a list, each use or application of it will be a review. After you've used the information the third or fourth time, no more review will be necessary. The ridiculous pictures will fade; you won't need them anymore. The memorized material will have become knowledge.

If you can remember a list of 10 items, you can remember a list of 15 or 16 items. If you can memorize 15 or 16, then you can memorize 25 or 26 items. There really is no limit.

Of course, it will take more time to Link 50 items than it does to Link 15 or 16. But it would take more time to remember 50 items whether or not you used the Link system!

Just in case you haven't realized it yet, trying to apply the Link system to a list of objects *forces* you to concentrate on two objects at a time in a way that you've never done before.

It forces Original Awareness. The information must register in your mind when you apply the system, and that's half the battle.

The Link system is used, basically, to help you remember things in sequence only. There are many kinds of information that must be memorized in sequence—at least at first, when you begin to study it. I'll be giving many examples of that in this book. Take my word for it at the moment—the Link system of memory will help immeasurably in your studies.

Learn it, practice it, understand it. Then, after you've tried it by yourself, a good way to continue to practice it is to demonstrate your new memory power for family and friends. Ask someone to call out a number of objects and have him write them down. Let him call out 15 or 16, or as many as you feel you can handle comfortably.

He has to write them down for two reasons. First, that's the only way he'll be able to check you when you call them off. Second, the writing gives you time to make good, strong associations. Later on you'll be able to make those associations almost as quickly as someone can call the objects.

After he has listed the 15 or 16 objects, you call them off, in sequence, from beginning to end. If you miss one or two, don't panic. Ask him to tell you what they were, strengthen that particular association, and then call them off backward. You'll really stun him! Try it and see.

Before you try it for other people, however, I'd suggest you try the practice lists at the end of the chapter. Also do the drills, and read the short Questions and Answers section.

Remember, you will have to understand the ideas thoroughly before you tackle your schoolwork. Although it will take some time for you to become thoroughly familiar with the ideas, in a short while they'll be saving you time. You have to learn these systems before they can help you to learn.

QUESTIONS AND ANSWERS:

If you have any questions in mind, perhaps they'll be answered here.

QUESTION: How do I remember the first item of a Link?

ANSWER: For the time being, you can associate it with yourself in some ridiculous way. That'll do it. Or associate the first item with the friend for whom you're "showing off." When we get to actual study material, you'll see how the main subject itself leads you into the Link. Of course, another way is simply to start at any item in the Link and work backward until you come to the first one.

QUESTION: Is it all right to form a "story" in my mind that Links the objects?

ANSWER: No! Each pair of objects should be handled as a separate entity. If you try to include all the items in one picture story, it may confuse you. Each association should concern itself with only the two vital items. Actually, a kind of story will form anyway, but always do it as I suggested, with a separate and distinct picture for each pair of items.

QUESTION: Is it the same thing simply to "think" the picture instead of trying to see it in my mind's eye?

ANSWER: It's better to make the slight effort to try to "see" the picture. That slight effort is what forces the Original Awareness. After a while, the effort won't be necessary. The truth of the matter is that "thinking" a picture is about the same as picturing it in your mind. It's almost impossible to think of anything without a picture of that thing flitting through your mind. Aristotle said it centuries ago: "In order to think we must speculate with images."

QUESTION: How many items can I remember with the Link system?

ANSWER: There's really no limit. One item must always lead you to the next one, if you have followed instructions.

QUESTION: Why must the pictures I form in my mind be ridiculous ones?

ANSWER: Mainly because forming a logical picture requires no thought. What you do not think of, for at least a second, cannot really be remembered. Trying to make the pictures ridiculous forces you to think of the items. It forces the Original Awareness. If you were to try to apply this system by using logical pictures, it would not work nearly so well.

QUESTION: How long can I retain a list that I've memorized via the Link system?

ANSWER: You can retain any list for as long as you want to or need to. We must assume that, except for practice, any list you memorize is to be used. It is the *use* that forces, or brings about, retention. Once the information is etched into your mind, once it becomes knowledge, the original associations or pictures fade. The information will stay with you for as long as you need it.

QUESTION: If I'm memorizing more than one list via the Link system and the same item appears in more than one list, will that confuse me?

ANSWER: You can remember as many lists as you want with the Link system of memory. The same item appearing in more than one list will not confuse you. You need only try it to see that this is so.

QUESTION: If I'm demonstrating the Link for a friend and he calls out abstract or intangible things, what do I do?

ANSWER: Tell him to call tangible items only. Don't let him control you—you control him. You're demonstrating for him, remember. If he doesn't want to call tangible things, just don't demonstrate for him; it's his loss. In a little while, however, you'll learn to handle intangible things just as easily as tangible things. Then it will be no problem.

HAVE SOME FUN; COMPLETE THESE DRILLS:

Following this paragraph are four lists of objects. Try to memorize each list using the Link system. Be sure to make the pictures ridiculous and to see each one in your mind's eye for at least a split second. To be sure the pictures are ridiculous, try to make them Out of Proportion or Exaggerated, or use Action or Substitution. I would also suggest that you do not try all the lists at one sitting.

drum	pin	snake	teabag
string	window shade	feather	soap
comb	desk	belt	telephone
key	glass	cup	foot
paint	flower	eyeglasses	garbage can
light bulb	pipe	building	dog
ice cube	stamp	ball	plate
picture frame	cat	cuff links	pen
cracker	record player	scale	gum
ring	pizza	horse	cards
chair		bed	lamppost
fish		doughnut	bottle
briefcase			sled
coin			paper bag
baby			dress
			fork
			magazine
			tree
			teeth
			airplane

After you've done those lists, make up your own and practice Linking. After that, you're ready to have a friend test you on a list that he or she makes up.

For this final drill, jot down three or four ridiculous pictures for each of the pairs of items listed. The purpose of this drill is to help you practice thinking up ridiculous pictures quickly.

It is also a great imagination exercise! Do not use any logical pictures.

If you'd like more practice after you've done the pairs below, simply move all the second items up one step. Then you'll be working with rock and microphone, toothbrush and guitar, and so on. Switch them any way you like in order to get different pairs of items. Be sure to complete the drill.

rock and book ..... *rock reading a book*

toothbrush and microphone ..... *a man using a toothbrush as a microphone*

pencil and guitar ..... *a pencil playing a guitar*

baseball bat and lamp ..... *a ball player using a lamp as a bat*

necktie and rubber band ..... *a giant rubber band wearing a necktie*

wheel and paper clip ..... *a paper clip turning a steering wheel*

tin can and ship ..... *ship floating in a giant tin can*

coffeepot and cigar ..... *a coffee pot smoking a cigar*

dollar bill and buzz saw ..... *a man sawing a tree with a dollar bill* scissors and bean *a giant bean cutting a piece of paper with scissors*

hair and blotter *a blotter with hair growing out of it*

marble and calendar *a calendar playing marbles*

cake and fishing rod *catching a giant cake with a fishing rod*

couch and newspaper *couch reading a newspaper*

letter and doorknob *doorknob writing a letter*

If you have completed these drills without too much trouble, then you're ready to continue. If you had a bit of trouble, I'd suggest you reread this chapter and try the drills again before going on.

6

THE PEG SYSTEM OF MEMORY
(THE PHONETIC ALPHABET)

Now, let's go a step further. The Link system is used to memorize things in sequence only. If you were asked for the, say, sixth item of a memorized Link, you wouldn't know it. You'd have to count forward in the Link to that item, and it's hardly worth that much time and effort.

The Peg system is used for just that reason—to allow you to memorize whatever you like in and out of order and by number. The basis of the Peg system is a phonetic (sound) alphabet. It is really quite simple and fascinating. Not only will it help you to remember items in and out of order; what is more important, it will also help you to memorize *all* numbers easily and quickly. We'll take it a step at a time.

There are ten digits in our numerical system—1, 2, 3, 4, 5, 6, 7, 8, 9, and 0. There are also only ten consonant phonetic sounds in our language.

Let me take a moment to explain that. I know that at first thought it would seem that there are more than ten consonant phonetic sounds in the English language.

But look at the letters *T* and *D*. Although they are two completely different letters, they make the same phonetic sound.

Here's a simple rule to help you understand when two or more letters make the same phonetic sound. If your lips, tongue, teeth, and the rest of your vocal apparatus are in the same position when you form two or more sounds, then the sounds are the same phonetically—at least they are the same for our purpose.

With *T* and *D* the tip of your tongue hits the back of your upper front teeth. Try it and see. The *T* sound is harder than the *D* sound, but they are the same phonetically.

If you understand that, then the rest is easy. *F* and *V* have the same phonetic sound. Your upper front teeth press against the inside of your lower lip for both of them. The *V* sound is softer than the *F* sound, but they are the same, phonetically.

P and *B* form the same phonetic sound. You purse your lips the same way for each one. *K,* hard *G* (as in "go"), and hard *C* (as in "coat") are the same hard, back-of-the-throat, phonetic sound.

J, SH, CH, and soft *G* (as in "giant") all have the same phonetic sound. So do *Z, S,* and soft *C* (as in "cent"). They are the "hissing" sounds.

There are only ten of these consonant phonetic sounds. What I have done is to pair them with the digits, and since the ten pairs of sounds and numbers will always remain the same, you'll always know them once you learn them.

They are easy to remember, but I'll make it even easier by giving you a little memory aid for each one. You will need this aid only at first. If you concentrate on the list and the silly little memory aids, you will most likely know all the sounds after one reading.

One thing you must understand—it is the sound the letters make that we are interested in, not the letters themselves. You'll soon see why that is so.

Number 1 will always be represented by the sounds made by the letters *T* and *D,* and vice versa. A little aid to help you remember it (only at first) is that the letter *T* has *one* downstroke.

Number 2 will always be represented by the sound of the letter *N.* The small letter *n* has *two* downstrokes.

Number 3 = *M*. The small letter *m* has *three* downstrokes. Or, if you put an *m* on its side, it looks like a 3; put a 3 on its side, and it looks like an *m*.

Number 4 = *R*. The only aid I can give you for this one is that the word "fou*R*" ends with the *R* sound. Or use a bit of imagination. Look at the *R*. Can you picture a golfer teeing off? And of course he's yelling, "Fore."

Number 5 = *L*. The Roman numeral for 50 is *L*. Or you can form the letter *L* with your 5 fingers. Hold your left hand with the palm out, as if you were saying, "Stop." Stick the thumb straight out. The hand looks like an *L*.

Number 6 = *J, SH, CH*, soft *G* (as in "gentleman"). The number 6 and the letter *J* are almost mirror images. That is, if you look at one in the mirror, it looks like the other (ϑ 6).

Number 7 = *K*, hard *C* (as in "crazy"), hard *G* (as in "great"). You can form a capital *K* with two sevens; one right side up and the other upside down (𝒦).

Number 8 = *F, V, PH* (as in "phony"). The number 8 and the small handwritten *f* are similar. That is, each one has two loops, one above the other (8 𝑓).

Number 9 = *P, B*. The letter *P* and the number 9 are almost exact mirror images. (*P9*).

0 = *S, Z*, soft *C* (as in "center"). The first sound in the word "zero" is Z.

The only consonant sound that is missing is the *TH* sound, as in "the." This sound will rarely come up, but for our purposes, it will be the same as *T* and represent number 1.

The vowels, *A, E, I, O,* and *U*, have no meaning or value in my phonetic alphabet. Neither do the letters *W, H,* and *Y* (easy to remember—the word "why").

The word "knee" would break down, or transpose, to number 2, not 72. Do you see why? It is the sound the letter makes that's important, not the letter itself. The *K* in the word "knee" is silent. It makes no sound; therefore, it has no numerical value. The only consonant sound in the word "knee" is the *N* sound, and that's number 2.

The word "climb" would break down, or transpose, to 753 —not 7539. The *B* is silent; therefore, it has no numerical value.

The same rule holds true for double letters. The word "butter" would transpose to the number 914—not 9114. Because, even though there are two *T*'s in the word, those *T*'s make only one *T* sound. The word "pillow" transposes to 95 because the double *L* makes a single *L* sound. This is so for all double letters. All right, then—

1 = T (or D)	—A *t* has *one* downstroke.
2 = N	—A small *n* has *two* downstrokes.
3 = M	—A small *m* has *three* downstrokes.
4 = R	—The word "fou*R*" ends with the *R* sound.
5 = L	—The Roman numeral for 50 is *L*.
6 = J (or SH, CH, soft G)	—A capital *J* is almost a mirror image of a 6 (J6).
7 = K (or hard C, hard G)	—A capital *K* can be formed with two 7's (𝒦).
8 = F (or V)	—A handwritten small *f* and an 8 have two loops, one above the other (8 f).
9 = P (or B)	—The letter *P* and the number 9 are almost exact mirror images (P9).
0 = S (or Z, soft C)	—The first sound in the word "zero" is Z.

The letter *Q* is pronounced like the letter *K*, so it represents 7. The letter *X* will never be used, but to make the list complete, it can represent 70 or 76, according to the way it is sounded in a word. For example, in the word "box" the *X* could be written *KS* because those are the sounds it makes, so it transposes to 70. In the word "anxious" the *X* could have been written *SH*, so it transposes to 76.

If you go over the sounds of the phonetic alphabet you'll see that you already know most of them. Just think of the little memory aid I gave you for each one. You should know them in and out of order, so that the sounds become second nature to you. They will be of more help to you than you can possibly realize now, and you'll use them for the rest of your life.

You can learn them as well as your ABC's by playing a simple game for just a short while. Whenever you see a number—on a license plate, in an address, for example—mentally try to transpose the numbers into sounds. Whenever you see a word on a sign or billboard, try to transpose the consonant sounds to numbers.

Here are some drills to start you off. Complete them all, fill in the blanks, and you'll be well on your way toward knowing the sounds perfectly. The answers follow the drills, just in case you want to check. Do not continue reading until you have completed these drills and know the phonetic alphabet.

R = ...　　P = ...　　Hard C (as in "cat") = ...
L = ...　　Hard G (as in "green") = ...　　B = ...
K = ...　　N = ...　　V = ...　　D = ...
J = ...　　Soft C (as in "cigar") = ...　　T = ...
M = ...　　Z = ...　　S = ...　　CH = ...

5 = L.　　1 = ...　　0 = ...　　8 = ...
4 = ...　　9 = ...　　2 = ...　　6 = ...
7 = ...　　3 = ...

436 = RMJ.　　729 = ...　　381 = ...
529 = ...　　123 = ...　　890 = ...　　567 = ...
345 = ...　　089 = ...　　553 = ...　　778 = ...
787 = ...　　877 = ...　　004 = ...　　400 = ...
040 = ...　　912 = ...　　823 = ...　　333 = ...

6214 = JNTR.　　53091 = ...　　26 = ...
935210 = ...　　481632 = ...　　24680 = ...
97531 = ...　　08 = ...　　213560 = ...
0011223 = ...　　911998 = ...

BUTTER = 914.　　　PATTER = ...　　　BITER = ...
TUB = ...　　BIDDER = ...　　BITE RYE = ...
TERROR = ...　　　BREAK = ...　　　VISION = ...
TELEPHONE = ...　　　CHANDELIER = ...
BOOKKEEPER = ...　　　BRINGING = . . 27 . . .
PACKAGING = ...　　　MELLOW = ...
PILLOW = ...　　PORCELAIN = ...
SCISSORS = ...　　MISSISSIPPI = ...
PHILADELPHIA = ...　　　TATTLE = ...
TAILORS = ...　　BIG DEAL = ...
CAREFUL = ...　　　LORAYNE = ...

Answers to Drill

R = 4.　　P = 9.　　Hard C = 7.　　L = 5.　　Hard G = 7.
B = 9.　　K = 7.　　N = 2.　　V = 8.　　D = 1.　　J = 6.
Soft C = 0.　　T = 1.　　M = 3.　　Z = 0.　　S = 0.
CH = 6.

5 = L.　　1 = T, D.　　O = S, Z, soft C.　　8 = F, V.
4 = R.　　9 = P, B.　　2 = N.　　6 = J, SH, CH, soft G.
7 = K, hard C, hard G.　3 = M.

436 = RMJ.　　729 = KNP.　　381 = MFT.
529 = LNP.　　123 = TNM.　　890 = FPS.　　567 = LJK.
345 = MRL.　　089 = SFP.　　553 = LLM.　　778 = KKF.
787 = KFK.　　877 = FKK.　　004 = SSR.　　400 = RSS.
040 = SRS.　　912 = PTN.　　823 = FNM.　　333 = MMM.

6214 = JNTR.　　53091 = LMSPT.　　26 = NJ.
935210 = PMLNTS.　　481632 = RFTJMN.
24680 = NRJFS.　　97531 = PKLMT.　　08 = SF.
213560 = NTMLJS.　　0011223 = SSTTNNM.
911998 = PTTPPF.

BUTTER = 914.　　PATTER = 914.　　BITER = 914.
TUB = 19.　　BIDDER = 914.　　BITE RYE = 914.

TERROR = 144.   BREAK = 947.   VISION = 862.
TELEPHONE = 1582.   CHANDELIER = 62154.
BOOKKEEPER = 9794.   BRINGING = 942727.
PACKAGING = 97627.   MELLOW = 35.
PILLOW = 95   PORCELAIN = 94052.
SCISSORS = 0040.   MISSISSIPPI = 3009.
PHILADELPHIA = 85158.   TATTLE = 115.
TAILORS = 1540.   BIG DEAL = 9715.
CAREFUL = 7485.   LORAYNE = 542.

If any of your answers did not match mine, I'd suggest you go back and find out why.

7

THE PEG SYSTEM OF MEMORY
(PEG WORDS)

If you know the sounds of the phonetic alphabet, you can make up a word or phrase to represent any number. That is of utmost importance because numbers are the most difficult things to remember. They are geometric designs. They have no meaning and can't be pictured in the mind, and anything that can't be pictured in the mind is extremely difficult to remember.

But now, knowing the sounds of the phonetic alphabet, you will be able to picture numbers. Now, if you want to remember, say, number 17, all you need is a word that will represent 17, a word that can be pictured. For example, *tack* can represent only number 17 in the phonetic alphabet.

You see why, don't you? The *T* sound is 1 and the *K* sound is 7. *T* + *K* = 17. Of course *T* + *K* would be as difficult to picture as 17, but the word "tack" is easy to envision. Therefore, picturing a tack in your mind is the same as picturing 17.

Knowing the ten phonetic sounds gives you a way to make any number meaningful. If you pictured a *red bag,* that would remind you of 4197. *Paper dog* could mean only 99417. And so on.

You can make up words as you need them, but it will save time if you have some words all ready. They will be called Peg Words. *Tack* is the Peg Word for 17.

Below are the Peg Words for numbers 1 through 10. After you see how easy it is, you will learn a fascinating use for those Peg Words.

For number 1, we need a word that has only *one* consonant sound, because 1 is a single digit. This one-consonant sound in the word must be *T* or *D,* for that is the sound that represents 1.

There are many words that would fit. The one I've selected is *Tie*. Tie could stand *only* for number 1, because it has only one consonant sound, the sound that represents number 1. It is also easy to picture. Therefore, the Peg Word for 1 is (and always will be) *Tie*.

The Peg Word for 2 must also have only one consonant sound, but for this number, the one sound must be *N*. I've selected the word (or name) *Noah*. For Noah, you can picture animals, the ark, or whatever you like. I simply picture an old man with a long gray beard. The Peg Word for 2 will always be *Noah*.

The Peg Word for 3 is *Ma* because it has only the *M* sound in it. Picture your mother for Ma, or a gray-haired lady.

For number 4, the Peg Word is *Rye*. Picture a loaf of rye bread (or a bottle of rye whiskey).

For number 5, the Peg Word is *Law*. I always picture a policeman, who represents the law, for this.

Number 6 = *Shoe*. Shoe can represent only number 6 because it has only the *SH* sound. Picture a shoe, of course.

Number 7 = *Cow*. Picture the animal.

Number 8 = *Ivy*. The sound *V* represents number 8. Picture ivy growing on walls.

Number 9 = *Bee*. Picture the stinging insect.

Number 10 = This number has two digits, a 1 and a 0, in that order. So we need a word that has both those consonant sounds, in that order. The word I've selected is *Toes*. The sounds tell you what number the word represents. *Toes* could represent only number 10.

If you know the sounds, you probably already know the first ten Peg Words. Look at them once more:

1. Tie	6. SHoe
2. Noah	7. Cow
3. Ma	8. iVy
4. Rye	9. Bee
5. Law	10. ToeS

Because you know the sounds in and out of order, you'll also know the Peg Words in and out of order. You should be fairly familiar with these first ten Pegs before you continue. See if you can fill in these blanks:

8 = ...   4 = ...   6 = . . .   3 = ...   10 = ...
2 = ...   5 = ...   7 = . .   9 = . . .   1 = . . .
Noah = ...   Bee = ...   Rye = . . .   Tie = ...
ToeS = ...   SHoe = ...   Law = ...   iVy = ...
Ma = . . .   Cow = ...

Now, what good do these Peg Words do you? Let me show you. Let's assume, just for demonstration purposes, that you had to remember ten things in and out of order and by number. To make it even more fun, let's also assume that you heard or read the items out of order.

For some reason, you want to remember that number 6 is an *envelope*. Now, usually, there'd be no problem picturing an envelope. But how in the world would you picture number 6? Ordinarily, you couldn't. But now you can! What is the Peg Word for 6? Easy! The sound for 6 is *SH*. This tells you that the Peg Word is shoe. Picturing a shoe is the same as picturing number 6.

So all you have to do is to make an association (just as you've already learned) between *shoe* and *envelope*. That's all. Be sure to make the picture ridiculous and see it clearly in your mind. You might see yourself wearing gigantic envelopes instead of shoes, or licking and sealing a shoe instead of an envelope. Or you might imagine a gigantic envelope wearing shoes and walking. Or perhaps you're mailing a shoe in an envelope. Select one and see that picture before you continue.

You might want to remember that number 2 is a *TV set*. What is your Peg Word for 2? Noah, right! Associate Noah with a TV set. You might see a TV set with a long gray beard, or picture an ark on top of your TV set. Select one, or one you thought of yourself, and, most important, see it in your mind.

Number 8 is a *wristwatch,* and the Peg Word for 8 is ivy. Form a ridiculous picture using wristwatch and ivy. You might see millions of wristwatches growing on a wall instead of ivy. Or see yourself wearing a bunch of ivy on your wrist instead of a watch. The picture you use is not important. What is important is that you see that picture clearly.

Number 4 is *briefcase,* and the Peg Word for 4 is rye. Picture yourself carrying a large loaf of rye bread instead of a briefcase. Or imagine that you're buttering and eating a briefcase instead of rye bread, or that you open a briefcase and millions of loaves of rye bread fly out, or that you're carrying rye whiskey in the briefcase. See the picture.

Number 9 is *lamp.* The Peg Word for 9 is bee. You can see millions of lamps (instead of bees) swarming over you and stinging you. Perhaps a gigantic bee lights up like a lamp, or a gigantic bee lights a lamp, or you light a lamp and millions of bees fly out and sting you.

Number 1 is *pen.* Your Peg Word for 1 is tie. You're wearing a gigantic pen around your neck instead of a tie. See the ink dripping on your shirt or dress and ruining it. Or you're writing on your tie with a pen. Picture whichever you think is more ridiculous.

Number 7 is *rope*, and the Peg Word for 7 is cow. Most often, I see the item I want to remember for 7 coming out of the cow's udders instead of milk. My picture for this would be that I'm milking a cow and ropes come out instead of milk.

Number 3 is *coin*, and your Peg Word is Ma. You might see your mother covered with coins, or your mother's picture might be on a coin. Perhaps you're buying something and you're paying with your mother instead of a coin. It doesn't matter how ridiculous you get. The more ridiculous, the better. Select one and see that picture.

Number 10 is *knife*. What's your Peg Word for 10? Toes, of course. You might see knives on your feet instead of toes, or picture knives between all your toes, cutting you. Select any ridiculous picture and see it for a split second.

Finally, number 5 is *ashtray*. The Peg Word for 5 is law. You can see a gigantic ashtray walking the beat like a policeman, or a gigantic ashtray being arrested by a policeman.

If you've really tried to see the pictures, you'll probably amaze even yourself.

Let's try it in order first. See if you can fill in these blanks from 1 to 10. All you have to do is think of your Peg Word for each number. That will tell you the item you want to remember. Since this is the first time you've tried this, the Peg Words are given in the first drill. When you've filled in the blanks, cover them with your hand and fill in the blanks in the second column.

1 (tie)	= . .	1.	
2 (Noah)	=	2.	
3 (Ma)	= . .	3. .	
4 (rye)	= . .	4.	
5 (law)	= . .	5.	

6 (shoe)	=	6.	....
7 (cow)	=	7.	....
8 (ivy)	=	8.	....
9 (bee)	=	9.	....
10 (toes)	=	10.	....

So far, however, you haven't done anything that's very different from the Link system. You've memorized ten items in order, although they were given to you out of order. But if you know your Peg Words, you also know the items out of order. That means that you know the position of any of the items. What was the item you remembered for number 6? Think of your Peg Word first. Shoe. What does shoe remind you of? Envelope, of course. It's as simple as that! Fill in the following blanks.

8.	....	10.	....
2.	....	7.	....
5.	....	4.	....
9.	....	6.	....
1.	....	3.	....

If you hear or read the item, you'll know its position! What position is the wristwatch? Well, what does wristwatch remind you of? Ivy, of course. Ivy is your Peg Word for 8, so wristwatch must be number 8. Fill in the following blanks.

rope =	....	briefcase =	....
knife =	....	wristwatch =	....
pen =	....	TV set =	....
lamp =	....	envelope =	....
ashtray =	....	coin =	....

You should be proud of yourself! You read ten items once, and you know them by number: forward, backward, and inside out!

But what would you do if you had to memorize eleven items, or twenty-five, or fifty? Although you can make up words or phrases to fit any number (as long as you know the sounds), it will save time to have some all ready. It's easy. If I told you to make up a word for number 74, you'd simply think of the proper sounds, *K* and *R*. Just say them to yourself: *K–R*. What word comes to mind? You probably thought of *car*—and that's the Peg Word for 74.

The word for 11 must have a *T* and *T* sound. The word is *tot*. Picture a baby. For 12 we must have a *T* or *D* and *N* sound, in that order. The word is *tin*. For number 12, picture anything you want to remember made out of tin. For number 13 we need a word that has the *T* and *M* sound, in that order. I've selected the word *tomb*. Don't let that *B* throw you; it's silent, so it has no value. The word tomb can represent only number 13. You can picture a gravestone for it, or Grant's Tomb.

Try to learn, say, ten at a time. It's fun, and it's easy. Below is a list of Peg Words from 1 to 100. If you don't feel like learning them all, at least learn 1 to 20 well. Familiarize yourself with the others. If you do learn them all, you'll be able to memorize a list of one hundred items in and out of order, by number. And, of course, the better you know the Peg Words, the faster you can do it.

All the words I've selected are easy to picture. After a while, you won't even have to think of the sounds; the picture of the thing the Peg Word represents will come instantly to mind when you hear or read the number.

1. tie	26. notch	51. lot	76. cage
2. Noah	27. neck	52. lion	77. coke
3. Ma	28. knife	53. limb	78. cave
4. rye	29. knob	54. lure	79. cob
5. law	30. mouse	55. lily	80. fez
6. shoe	31. mat	56. leech	81. fat
7. cow	32. moon	57. log	82. phone
8. ivy	33. mummy	58. lava	83. foam
9. bee	34. mower	59. lip	84. fur
10. toes	35. mule	60. cheese	85. file

11. tot	36. match	61. sheet	86. fish
12. tin	37. mug	62. chain	87. fog
13. tomb	38. movie	63. jam	88. fife
14. tire	39. mop	64. cherry	89. fob (or fib)
15. towel	40. rose	65. jail	90. bus
16. dish	41. rod	66. choo choo	91. bat
17. tack	42. rain	67. chalk	92. bone
18. dove	43. ram	68. chef	93. bum
19. tub	44. rower	69. ship	94. bear
20. nose	45. roll	70. case	95. bell
21. net	46. roach	71. cot	96. beach
22. nun	47. rock	72. coin	97. book
23. name	48. roof	73. comb	98. puff
24. Nero	49. rope	74. car	99. pipe
25. nail	50. lace	75. coal	100. disease (or dozes)

If you learn the Pegs from 1 to 20 well, you can really show off. Have someone number a paper from 1 to 15 or from 1 to 20 (as many as you feel you can handle comfortably), and let him call a number and an object, in any order. As he calls each object, he writes it next to the number called. You make the associations as you've learned.

When every number has an object, you call the objects off from 1 to the end. Then, let him call any number and you tell him the object. After that, let him call any object and you tell him the number! You're a memory expert already!

Even though you may not have to remember anything in and out of order, by number, for your schoolwork, it is handy to know the Peg system and the phonetic alphabet. You do have to remember numbers in your studies.

Before you continue to the next chapter, read the Questions and Answers section below and complete the drills.

QUESTIONS AND ANSWERS:

QUESTION: Why is the phonetic alphabet based on the sounds and not the letters?
ANSWER: Because, being based on the sounds, the system

works even if a person can't read or speak well! Also, many letters in our alphabet make different sounds in different words. There's an old joke that says that one way to spell fish is ghoti.

Here's why: *GH* as in couGH, *O* as in wOmen, and *TI* as in naTIon. So remember, it's the sound the letter makes that's important, not the letter itself.

QUESTION: Can I change some of the Peg Words to words I like better?

ANSWER: I wouldn't suggest you do it until you've finished this book. Later on, I'll be giving you other Peg lists. If you change any of your basic Peg Words now, they may conflict with some of those words, and that could cause confusion. After you've learned those lists you can change any words you want to change, as long as the words you use can be pictured and each one fits its number phonetically.

The words I've given you are all easy to picture in the mind. It really doesn't matter what the word is; it's the picture it conjures up in your mind that's important.

QUESTION: Would it confuse me if I memorized more than one list using the Peg system?

ANSWER: No, of course not. "True" memory will tell you which Peg list you're working with at any particular time. Also, remember that once you've locked any information into your memory the original associations fade while the information remains.

You'll seldom confuse lists even though you have used the same Peg Words to memorize them originally. You'll see that this is so when you try it.

QUESTION: Why must the Peg Words fit the phonetic alphabet? Couldn't I use *any* words to represent certain numbers?

ANSWER: Sure you could, but then you'd be using rote memory to remember the words in the first place. The whole point of this book is to eliminate rote memory, not to find uses for it!

Besides, you'd have nothing to remind you of a Peg Word

if you used just any word. With the phonetic system, once you know only ten sounds, it's easier to remember the Peg Words than it is to forget them. If one should slip your mind, simply add vowel sounds after, or between, the consonant sounds, and before you know it, the word will come to mind.

QUESTION: Should I link the Peg Words to help me remember them?

ANSWER: No. Don't create problems where none exist. It isn't necessary at all; the sounds are the only aids you need. Not only that, but the Peg Words must be known out of order. That's the whole point. The Link system is only for memorizing things in sequence.

QUESTION: Must my pictures for the Peg system be ridiculous?

ANSWER: Always try to make the pictures as ridiculous as possible. That is very important; it is what forces the Original Awareness. After a while, you'll think of ridiculous associations easily. Before you know it, a ridiculous or impossible picture incorporating any two objects will come to mind before a logical one does. This also holds true for the Link system.

QUESTION: What do I do if more than one ridiculous picture runs through my mind for an association?

ANSWER: Don't worry about it. Just try to see one of them clearly.

Here's a drill on the Peg Words from 1 to 100. Try it after you've gone over all the words once or twice. Try to fill in every blank.

65 = jail	bear = ...	35 = ...	neck = ...
96 = ...	tack = ...	66 = ...	lot = ...
8 = ...	lure = ...	foam = ...	36 = ...
49 = ...	mummy = ...	tire = ...	91 = ...
42 = ...	86 = ...	pipe = ...	tin = ...
rye = ...	1 = ...	46 = ...	23 = ...
100 = ...	bus = ...	moon = ...	bell = ...
nose = ...	85 = ...	leech = ...	67 = ...
2 = ...	89 = ...	cob = ...	notch = ...

limb = ...	mouse = ...	92 = ...	31 = ...
16 = ...	21 = ...	fife = ...	rower = ...
sheet = ...	cave = ...	55 = ...	coke = ...
93 = ...	15 = ...	lava = ...	37 = ...
5 = ...	10 = ...	75 = ...	puff = ...
73 = ...	94 = ...	6 = ...	mop = ...
jam = ...	52 = ...	Ma = ...	knife = ...
65 = ...	59 = ...	97 = ...	7 = ...
40 = ...	fez = ...	69 = ...	72 = ...
ram = ...	19 = ...	nail = ...	cherry = ...
76 = ...	38 = ...	9 = ...	fat = ...
68 = ...	74 = ...	34 = ...	roof = ...
fog = ...	84 = ...	57 = ...	11 = ...
22 = ...	phone = ...	60 = ...	24 = ...
roll = ...	62 = ...	dove = ...	rod = ...
29 = ...	71 = ...	13 = ...	70 = ...
	47 = ...	50 = ...	

If you've filled in all the blanks, then you know your Peg Words pretty well. The more you use them, the better you'll know them.

Try to memorize the fifteen objects in the list below. Make the associations in the order given in the left column. In other words, the object to memorize for number 12 (tin) is *drapes.* Associate tin with drapes. Then associate Ma to *microphone,* and so on. When you've made all the associations, cover the left column with your hand or a piece of paper and try to fill in all the blanks in the second column.

When you've done that, cover the first two columns and see if you can fill in the blanks in column three. Finally, cover the first three columns and see how quickly you can fill in the blanks in the last column.

When you want to remember numbers with more than two digits, perhaps three or four digits, you can simply associate two Peg Words to remind you of those digits. For instance, for a date like 1819, a picture of a gigantic *dove* (18) in a *tub* (19) would do the trick.

But you don't have to use the Peg Words. Usually, for a three- or four-digit number, it is better to make up a word or phrase

12. drapes	1. noodle
3. microphone	2. PILLOW
10. radio	3. MICROPHONE
7. lamppost	4. BOOK
2. pillow	5. MATTRESS
11. sword	6. CHEESE
5. mattress	7. LAMPPOST
9. spoon	8. CIGAR
15. sweater	9. SPOON
1. noodle	10. RADIO
4. book	11. SWORD
13. baseball bat	12. DRAPES
8. cigar	13. BASEBALL BAT
6. cheese	14. FLAG
14. flag	15. SWEATER

sword 11		5. mattress	
book 4		flag. 14	
cigar 8		9. SPOON	
drapes 12		microphone. 3	
flag 14		1. NOODLE	
lamppost 7		cheese. 6	
cheese 6		15. SWEATER	
baseball bat 13		sword. 11	
pillow 2		7. LAMPPOST	
spoon 9		drapes. 12	
microphone 3		2. PILLOW	
mattress 5		cigar. 8	
noodle 1		13. BASEBALL BAT	
sweater 15		book. 4	
radio 10		10. RADIO	

to cover all the digits. You'll be exercising your imagination, and you won't be using the same Peg Words so often.

Remember that a phrase consisting of two or more words is still usually only one picture in your mind. See if you can come up with the three or four words or phrases for each of the following numbers. Then check your answers with mine.

3624 ....
8270 ....
2120 ....
4215 ....
7214 ....

3624—missionary; matchin' her; mission rye; my shiner; imagine hair; ma join her; imaginary.
8270—fangs; fungus; fine kiss; ivy nicks; fine keys; view necks; vine gas.
2120—knot nose; end noose; no dance; no dunce; hen dunes; indians; no tines.
4215—ruin tail; ruined all; rye nettle; ran doll; rained eel; runt hill; rental; errand hill.
7214—counter; cantor; count rye; gained hair; kinder; candor; gowned her.

If you know your sounds, and if you use just a little bit of imagination, there is no three- or four-digit number for which you can't come up with a word or phrase that fits phonetically.

Anything can be pictured. It doesn't have to be an object; you can picture an action or a situation. As one example, you might look at 7321 and come up with *command*. How do you picture command? You might imagine an officer in the army commanding his men. Picture anything that would remind you of the word.

And if you come up with a word or phrase that you think you can't picture, just change it to something you can picture. For 7321, you could also use cow mount, come nut, comb net, common tea, cow moon tie, cow maned, come into, game nut, or commando.

8

THE SUBSTITUTE WORD SYSTEM OF MEMORY

If you could learn only one of the three basic ideas or systems of memory, I would probably suggest the Substitute Word idea. All three systems are important, of course, and sometimes you'll be using all of them to help you remember certain facts or information.

The Substitute Word idea is of utmost importance because it will help you to remember intangible information, information that cannot ordinarily be pictured in the mind—the most difficult information to remember.

How would you go about memorizing names—names of people, places, and things? It's easy, not to mention interesting and challenging, when you use the Substitute Word system of memory. The same system will make it easy and interesting to remember technical or scientific terminology and foreign or English vocabulary!

Let's take it a step at a time. First, what exactly is the Substitute Word idea? All it really means is that whenever you come upon a piece of information that you must memorize but cannot picture, make up a word or phrase that *sounds like* that information and that *can* be pictured!

I've done the same thing, really, with numbers. Numbers are completely abstract, but the phonetic alphabet helps make them meaningful.

The Substitute Word idea can be applied to anything. Perhaps the best way to explain it is to give a few basic examples.

Assume that you didn't know, and wanted to remember, that the word *barbecue* means an outdoor cooking grill or framework. What does barbecue sound like? Well, *barber Q* or *barber cue* would certainly remind you of it. If you saw a silly picture in your mind of a barber working on a gigantic letter *Q*, or on a cue stick, as the *Q* or cue roasted in an open grill, that would do it. That association would remind you of both the pronunciation of the word and its meaning.

To *plagiarize* is to steal someone else's ideas. Form this ridiculous picture in your mind: You have this great idea of playing with your eyes (*played your eyes*—plagiarize). Actually see yourself playing with them. Then everybody else starts doing the same thing. They've stolen your idea.

Yes, it's silly, but that's the point. If you had really wanted to learn those words, applying this idea would have forced you to concentrate on pronunciation and definition for at least a second or two; it would have forced Original Awareness. And the association has "locked" the information into your memory. If you hear, read, or think of the word, the definition will come to mind. On the other hand, if you think of the definition, the word will instantly come to mind. It works; it works better than you can possibly imagine at this moment. We'll really start applying the idea in the next chapter.

9

HOW TO REMEMBER
ENGLISH VOCABULARY

Let's see how well the Substitute Word system works with un-
familiar English words, for they can be as hard to remember
as foreign words. You may already know some of the examples I'll be using, but that doesn't really matter. The important thing is to understand the idea.

All it takes is a bit of imagination. For instance, the word
abeyance means "to hold in temporary suspension." Your
Substitute Word or thought for abeyance might be ants baying at
the moon (*bay ants*—abeyance) or a bay full of ants. If you
formed a ridiculous mental picture of ants baying, and being
temporarily suspended in the air while doing so, that would
do it. You'd have a reminder of the word itself and of its
meaning. Thinking of either would automatically bring the
other to mind.

Paleontology is the study of animal and plant fossils. A large
letter *E* is pale (*pale E*) and it is standing on top of a tall
G (*pale E on tall G*). It is standing on the tall *G* in order to
study animal and plant fossils. See the picture.

To *immigrate* is to move to a new place or residence. See
yourself pointing to a friend and saying, ungrammatically,
"Him and I are great" (*him, I, great*—immigrate). You and
your friend are continually moving from place to place. Be
sure to see the picture in your mind.

There are many substitute words that fit in each case. As an
example, for immigrate you might have pictured *a MIG* (a
Russian airplane) being *great,* and continually moving from
place to place. You can use my suggestions or think up your

own substitute words and silly associations. The system works much better, in fact, when you do your own thinking and use your own imagination. That's the whole point, really. When *you* think up the Substitute Word, you're forcing yourself to concentrate on the word you want to memorize. When you think up your own ridiculous picture, you're concentrating on the meaning and locking both word and meaning into your memory.

Apply the system and try to remember the following words and their meanings:

To *castigate* means to criticize, scold, or punish. Picture someone *casting a gate* and being *criticized* and/or *punished*.

Execrate means to abhor; detest. Your job is to put *eggs* into a *crate; you detest* doing it. See that picture.

An *endocarp* is the stone or pit of certain fruits (e.g., peach pit). You're hitting a carp (fish) with a gigantic *fruit pit.* That's the *end o'* the *carp.*

Hirsute means hairy. Picture yourself seeing a girl wearing a suit; you're pointing at *her suit* because it's covered with *hair.*

A *peduncle* is a flower stalk. See yourself having *paid* your *uncle* with *flower stalks* instead of money.

Benadryl is a drug used to relieve hay fever. You're *bend-ing a drill* and swallowing it, which causes you to *stop sneezing.*

Impeccable means faultless. Picture a man packing a bull (*him pack a bull*—impeccable) perfectly, without error—*faultlessly.* Really see that picture in your mind.

A *litany* is a type of prayer. You lit (burned) your knee (*lit a knee*) and you're saying a *prayer* over it.

Misanthrope—hater of mankind. Somebody is throwing something at all men, because he is a *hater of mankind,* and he misses his throw (*missin' throw*—misanthrope). Or, you could have used *missin' rope* or *miss ant rope.* Somebody is so mad at mankind that he's throwing a rope at an ant, and missing.

Vertigo—dizziness. You're getting *dizzy* trying to decide *where to go.*

Saturnine—gloomy. Picture yourself having *sat on* a gigantic number *nine* and you're very sad and *gloomy* about it. Or the number nine is gloomy.

Resupinate—bent backward. See yourself *bending backward* in order to read soup (alphabet soup?), then you ate it (*read soup and ate*).

Subsidy—financial aid. A *sub* (submarine) comes into the *city* to seek *financial aid.*

If you've formed the associations and reviewed them once or twice, you should know the meaning of each of these words: barbecue, plagiarism, abeyance, paleontology, immigrate, castigate, execrate, endocarp, hirsute, peduncle, Benadryl, impeccable, litany, misanthrope, vertigo, saturnine, resupinate, and subsidy.

It's important now for you to try a few words on your own. Try the words and definitions listed below. You're usually better off using the first Substitute Word or thought that comes to mind because that is the one that will come to mind first when you read or hear that word again. Make your associations ridiculous, see them clearly, and you'll learn these words faster and better than ever before.

abnegate—to renounce

brummagem—showy but inferior and worthless

lachrymose—tearful

anatine—resembling a duck

rapacity—greediness

obdurate—stubborn; hard

hexapod—having six feet

feasible—workable

agglutinate—thicken

obfuscate—confuse; make obscure

anchorite—hermit

encroach—to infringe

sycophant—flatterer

adminicle—an aid

colligate—arrange in order

effete—exhausted; worn out

alacrity—speed

culpable—guilty; deserving of blame

baneful—destructive

dilemma—perplexing situation

You can also apply the Substitute Word idea to prefixes (beginnings of words), stems (bodies of words), and suffixes (endings of words) as well as to full words. Obviously, if you know the meanings of these parts, it will serve as a memory aid toward knowing whole words. I don't want to list all the prefixes, stems, and suffixes here but if you want to apply the system to them, I'm sure you know where to find them.

Here are just a few examples; most of them are pretty obvious. For example, the prefix *sub* means *under*. Picturing a *sub*marine going *under* water is all you need. Just make it ridiculous in some way. The prefix *per* means *through*. See yourself walking *through* a gigantic *pear*. The prefix *poly* means *many*. Just picture *many pollies* (parrots). The prefix *ex* means *out*. See yourself Xing something *out*.

The stem *chron* means *time*. Picture a king wearing a clock (time) instead of a *crown*. The stem *clam* means *to shout*. See and hear a *clam shouting*. The stem *culp* means *to blame*. Someone is *blaming* you for something, and it makes you *gulp*. The stem *belli* means *war*. Picture a *war* being fought on your *belly*. The stem *rupt* means *to break*. Picture yourself having *rubbed* something in order *to break* it. Or a volcano is about to *erupt,* so you break it.

The suffix *ward* means *in the direction of*. Picture an entire hospital *ward* moving in your *direction*. The suffix *ose* or *ous* means *full of* or *given to*. See a *house* crammed full of anything being *given to* you. The suffix *atrist* means *one who practices*. Picture yourself *practicing a twist,* or *at* your *wrist*.

Well, if you've tried to apply the system to all the examples in this chapter, then you know how well the system works. It doesn't matter how difficult or strange a new word seems; simply apply the Substitute Word system and the word and its meaning will be easy to remember.

To repeat the advice given in the chapter on the Link and Peg systems, after you have applied the Substitute Word system to any word, and after you have relied on the system to remind you of a word and its meaning once or twice, the original association will fade. It will not run through your mind forever. The systems are a means to an end; once the end is accomplished or reached—once the word has become knowledge, once it has been learned—the means are no longer necessary.

Questions and answers pertaining to the Substitute Word idea are at the end of the next chapter.

10

FOREIGN LANGUAGE VOCABULARY

Many of my students have told me that one of the most fascinating and useful applications of the Substitute Word idea is in memorizing foreign language vocabulary. Once you understand the idea, you can memorize twenty, thirty, or more foreign words and their English meanings every day. You can memorize them quickly and easily, and you can retain them for as long as you like! You already understand the idea because it is applied to foreign vocabulary exactly as it is applied to English vocabulary.

For example, the Spanish word for bird is *pajaro,* pronounced pa-kar-o. That *K* sound is sometimes pronounced as an *H,* or as a back-of-the-throat *CH* sound. If you pronounce any of my examples differently from the way I'm suggesting, simply work accordingly. I'm interested only in teaching you the idea; once you understand that, you can handle any word or phrase.

How can you remember *pajaro* and also the fact that it means bird? Simply apply the Substitute Word idea exactly as you did for English words. First, try to think of something that sounds like pa-kar-o. That's pretty easy because the word almost sounds like *parked car.*

Parked car is tangible and can be pictured in your mind, and is enough to remind you of *pajaro.* To make sure you remember the meaning of the word, make a ridiculous or illogical association, just as you have been doing, between *parked car* and *bird.*

Again, the picture *you* think of is usually best. Again, there are many ways to picture it. You might imagine a parked car just stuffed full of birds, or you might see a bird parking a car or a car parked on top of a gigantic bird.

I assure you that if you see a ridiculous picture in your mind of a parked car and a bird, you'll always remember that the word *pajaro* means bird, and vice versa. As with English vocabulary, after you use a word two or three times, the silly picture will fade; you won't need it anymore. The information will have become knowledge!

By the way, don't worry about accents for any of these words for the moment. The important thing is to have a *reminder*.

The Spanish word *hermano* (pronounced air-mon-o) means brother. *Airman* would be a good Substitute Word. Form a ridiculous picture of *brother* and *airman*. Your brother—and if you don't have a brother, picture a boy who looks like you; it will still work—is an airman; perhaps he's flying a large letter *O* instead of a plane; airman *O—hermano*. See the picture.

Ventana means window in Spanish. You might picture a girl, whose name is *Anna,* throwing a *vent* (air conditioner) through a closed window. Vent Anna—*ventana*. Use this, or one you have thought of, and see it in your mind's eye.

Pluma is the Spanish word for pen. You're writing with a gigantic *plume* instead of a pen; *plumber, plum,* or *blue Ma* would also do. See the picture you select.

Toronja is the Spanish word for grapefruit. *Tear on jaw* sounds like toronja. You can picture a tear on your jaw and a gigantic grapefruit (or a million of them) coming out of that tear. Or a gigantic grapefruit has a tear on its jaw, or it's putting a tear on your jaw. See one of those ridiculous pictures in your mind's eye.

Mariposa is the Spanish word for butterfly. Picture a girl, whose name is *Mary, posing* while a gigantic butterfly lands on her head. If you like, instead of Mary, you can see a girl in a wedding gown, to represent *marry;* Mary (or marry) poser—*mariposa.* Or you can picture a gigantic butterfly posing as it is being married. As I've said, it doesn't matter how silly you get.

Harra is the Spanish word for water pitcher. Associate *horror* or *hairy* (or *airy*) with water pitcher. If you are studying Spanish, you know that the *h* in *harra* is silent.

Desperador is the Spanish word for alarm clock. *Desperate door* or *this pair o' doors* would do as Substitute Words or phrases; so would *this pear* (is) *a door*, or the words *desperado* or *desperate*. Associate alarm clock with any of these items. You might picture a gigantic alarm clock being a door, and it is desperate to get away; or a pair of alarm clocks are forming a door, and you're asking someone, "This pair a door?" See (and hear) the alarms ringing to get action into your picture.

Estrella (pronounced eh-stray-a) is the Spanish word for star. You might decide to picture a gigantic letter *S straying* (the *S* is a *strayer*) all the way to a star. Even if you imagined an *S* being a *sprayer* (*S* spraying a star) it would still remind you of the correct word and pronunciation.

Pantufla is the Spanish word for slipper. You could picture a gigantic *pan* trying (or preparing) *to fly;* or two pans are about to fly. *Pan to fly; pan two fly—pantufla.* With either one, associate slipper. You might see yourself wearing pans instead of slippers, and the pans are about to fly, or a slipper is the passenger in a pan that's about to fly.

Have you tried to see all the pictures? If you have, you should have no trouble filling in these blanks. If you haven't, go back and do it now; then fill in the blanks. And do yourself a favor; don't continue until you understand everything we've discussed up to now.

estrella means	toronja means
pluma means	hermano means
pantufla means	pajaro means
mariposa means	desperador means
ventana means	harra means

Now try it this way (fill in the Spanish word):

butterfly	. . . . . .	alarm clock	. .
window	. . . . . .	bird	. . . . .
slipper	. . . . .	star	. . . . . .
water pitcher	. . . . . .	pen	. . . . . .
brother	. . . . . .	grapefruit	. . . . . .

Do you see how simple it is? And do you see that the idea works immediately? What it's doing basically is forcing you to concentrate as you never have been able to before; it is forcing you to be Originally Aware.

Let's try just a few French words. The French word for bridge is *pont*. You might see yourself *punt*ing a bridge instead of a football, or punting a football over a bridge. Use whichever you like, but be sure to see the picture.

Père means father. Picture a large *pear* (the fruit) being your father.

Bouchon is the French word for cork. *Push on* or *bush on* would do it. See yourself *pushing on* a gigantic cork, or a *bush* is growing *on* a gigantic cork, or you're saying *"boo"* to a gigantic cork because it *shone* a light on you.

A grapefruit in France is a *pamplemousse*. Sounds difficult, doesn't it? If you picture a *moose* (or a *mouse*) with large *pimples* all over it, and those pimples are all grapefruits, it's easy.

The French word for heel is *talon*. The English word "talon" means a claw. So you can see a gigantic claw growing out of your heel, or something growing *tall on* your heel. Either one will do. We are not, of course, discussing pronunciation here. If you are studying a foreign language, then you'll know how certain letters are pronounced. What you are doing here is learning to remember the foreign word and its English equivalent.

The French word for squirrel is *écureuil*. *Egg cure oil* is pretty close to the sound of the word; close enough to remind you of it, even though the final l is not pronounced. A ridiculous picture of a squirrel laying an *egg* that runs over to some *oil* in order to *cure* it, will remind you of the word and the meaning.

If you've seen the pictures, you should have no trouble filling in these blanks:

bouchon means	....	père means	.....
pamplemousse means	....	pont means	.. ..
talon means	....	écureuil means	.....

Now try filling in the French words:

bridge	....	grapefruit	.. ....
father	....	heel	....
cork	....	squirrel	....

I think I've proved the point to you. More important, if you made the associations and filled in all the blanks, you've proved it to yourself. If you go back to the last chapter, you'll see that you still know the English words to which you applied the system.

If you want to remember the articles (feminine or masculine) in any foreign language, simply make up a word to represent one of them all the time. The masculine article in Spanish is *el,* the feminine, *la.* Remembering whether a noun is masculine or feminine in Spanish is easy since most of the feminine nouns end with an *a.* Therefore, if you make up a standard Substitute Word to represent either one, and always put that into that your pictures, that would do it.

For example, an elevated train is called an el. Simply stick an el (train) into your picture when you're memorizing a masculine noun. When you see that picture again, you'll know that the noun is masculine. If there's no train (el) in your picture, then the noun is feminine.

In French, the articles are *le* (masculine) and *la* (feminine). Do the same thing. Let's say you decide that the standard picture for *la* will be singing (la, la, la). When you form an association for a feminine noun, simply see one of the things in that association *singing*.

Pamplemousse is feminine. See the pimples (grapefruits) on the moose singing. That's all. If there is no singing in an association, then you'll know the noun is masculine.

There are other ways, of course. For example, you might get a dress into any association for a feminine noun, in any language, or get a lady or a man into the picture, accordingly. That's all you have to do. If there's a dress in the association, the noun is feminine; if there's no dress, the noun is masculine.

If you'd like some practice, below are eight Spanish words and eight French words. The Spanish words are pronounced just about as they're spelled. I'll give you the approximate pronunciation of the French words.

See if you can some up with a Substitute Word or phrase for each one. Then associate your Substitute Word with the English equivalent. In other words, apply the system and memorize the words as you have been doing. After you have made the associations test yourself. If you want to compare your Substitute Words and associations with mine, I'll give you an example of what I might have used for each one, but don't look at my suggestions until after you've tried your own.

Spanish	*French*
pelota—ball	*escargot* (ess-car-go)—snail
cuadro—picture	*cicatrice* (see-ka-treess)—scar
luz (looz)—light	*ongle* (ohngl)—fingernail
dinero—money	*citron* (sit-ron)—lemon
corbata—necktie	*échelle* (eh-shehl)—ladder
preguntar—(to) ask	*pomme* (pum)—apple
correr—(to) run	*fenêtre* (fuh-netr)—window
cantar—(to) sing	*manche* (mawnsh)—sleeve

Here's how I might have remembered the above words:

Pelota—ball. A *pail o' tar* is playing *ball*.

Cuadro—picture. A s*quad* is *row*ing a gigantic *picture* instead of a rowboat.

Luz—light. A gigantic *light* bulb is *loose* and falls, or you *lose* a gigantic *light* bulb.

Dinero—money. You're eating *money* for *dinner*. You can, if you like, see the money shaped like an *O,* or you might be saying, "Oh." Or perhaps an arrow is causing a din (noise) and you give it *money* to stop (*din arrow*—*dinero*).

Corbata—necktie. There's a large apple *core* around your neck instead of a *necktie* and you're hitting it with a *bat*.

Preguntar—to ask. You're *pray*ing to a *gun* that's covered with sticky *tar* and *asking* it questions.

Correr—to run. An apple *core* is *running* in mid*air*, or a man is coring gigantic pieces of fruit (he's a *corer*) and *running* as he does it.

Cantar—to sing. You're *tear*ing a tin *can* because it's *singing* loudly.

Escargot—snail. A gigantic *snail* that's shaped like a letter *S* gets into a *car* and makes it *go*.

Cicatrice—scar. You *see* a gigantic *car* among the *trees*, crashing into them and causing scars, or a large letter *C* is cutting rice (*C cut rice*—*cicatrice*) and causing *scars*.

Ongle—fingernail. A gigantic *fingernail* is your *uncle*; or your *fingernail* is very big and it's bent up at an *angle*.

Citron—lemon. Picture a gigantic *lemon* sitting and running at the same time. (*Sit run*—*citron*.)

Échelle—ladder. *A shell* is climbing a *ladder*, or a large letter *A* is carrying a *shell* and climbing a *ladder*.

Pomme—apple. See a gigantic *apple* with *pom*poms all over it, or you're *pum*meling (beating) an *apple*.

Fenêtre—window. See a fan eating (or having eaten) a raw window (*fan ate raw*—*fenêtre*).

Manche—sleeve. See yourself *munch*ing on a gigantic

sleeve. (Make it a *dress* sleeve, and you'll know that the word is feminine.) Or a gigantic *sleeve* is *munch*ing on you. Or it's early in the morning and a *sleeve* is making a lot of noise; you're saying to the sleeve, "It's *morn, sh!*"

It doesn't matter how long the word is. There's a Greek word that means *ant hole*. Actually, it translates to "worm and ant hole." This is the way a Greek man spelled it for me: *skoulikomermigotripa*. This word would seem impossible—or at least formidable—to remember. I simply broke it down (phonetically) this way: school, lea, core, mermaid, got ripper.

I pictured ant holes attending *school;* the school was in a *lea* (meadow); the lea was covered with apple *cores*; a *mermaid* was eating the cores; somebody approached to rip the mermaid, but she *got* the *ripper*.

Forming this simple Link made it easy for me to remember the word and its meaning. You can use any words you like, as long as they remind you of the sound. I used *core* where I did because that syllable is pronounced that way, rather than rhyming with "go." Instead of *got ripper* you could use *got rip Pa* or *go trip her;* instead of *mermaid,* you could use *murmer*. Whatever you think of is best for you.

At first, you'd hesitate a bit as you said the word. But assuming you're memorizing it because you intend to use it, you'll say it without hesitation after the third or fourth time. I know that if you woke me up at four A.M. and asked me to tell you the Greek word for ant hole, I'd instantly say, "skoulikomermigotripa."

Please understand that if the Substitute Word, phrase, or thought is not exactly like the word you're trying to remember, it doesn't really matter. "True" memory will tell you the exact sound of the word. Remember that all my systems are merely aids to your true memory. Applying one or all of the systems forces you to concentrate on the information; then it reminds you of it!

The head of a high school language department told me that one major memory problem for students of French, besides the vocabulary, is the problem of remembering the sixteen common nonreflexive verbs that are conjugated with *être* rather than *avoir*.

This is a pure and unadulterated memory problem; you either memorize the verbs or you don't. Of course, if you don't, you'll have some difficulty passing exams and the course of study itself.

Here are the sixteen verbs and their meanings:

descendre—to go down	*venir*—to come
devenir—to become	*rentrer*—to come back; reenter
entrer—to enter	*retourner*—to return; revisit
partir—to leave	*tomber*—to fall
aller—to go	*mourir*—to die
arriver—to arrive	*monter*—to go up; climb
rester—to remain; stay	*naître*—to be born
revenir—to come back (again)	*sortir*—to go out; leave

One teacher told me that she tells her students to remember the word "departments" because the letters of that word could (perhaps) remind them of the verbs. But it's not definite enough.

A student advised me that his teacher told his class to think of a house, because most of the actions could take place in a house. You are *born* in a house and *die* in a house, you *return* to a house and *enter* and *leave* a house, and so on. Again, it is not definite enough.

Assuming that you already know the meanings of the sixteen words, and that being reminded of the English meanings is tantamount to knowing the French words, a simple Link will do the trick. The house idea will do as well as anything.

Start the Link with a Substitute Word or phrase that will remind you of *être; eat raw* would suffice.

The Link that first came to my mind is the one in the next paragraph. It must have worked for me because I now know the sixteen verbs. It's almost a logical Link, so it's up to you to make it as ridiculous as possible. I'll give you only the basic idea. Here's the Link:

You're *eat*ing a large chunk of *raw* meat as you *come* (*venir*) to a gigantic house; you *enter* (*entrer*) it; you *go down* (*descendre*) a long flight of stairs in order to get some more raw meat; you *fall down* (*tomber*) the stairs; you *climb up* (*monter*) again and *leave* (*partir*) the house; someone shouts, "*Come back again*" (*revenir*), so you *reenter* (*rentrer*); you *go* (*aller*) to the staircase again just as someone *arrives* (*arriver*) and *becomes* (*devenir*) very angry; you are frightened and know that if you *remain* (*rester*), you will *die* (*mourir*), so you *go out* (*sortir*) into the fresh air and feel as if you've been *born* (*naître*) again; you vow that you'll never *return* (*retourner*) to that house.

Go over this Link a few times, really see those pictures, and you'll know the sixteen verbs that are conjugated with *être*. There are some shades of difference in some of the meanings as I've used the words but, again, that's not important here. The assumption is that you know the exact meanings; it's the reminder that's important. If you pictured the raw meat in a *dish* (Peg Word for 16) that would serve to remind you that there are sixteen of the verbs—if you feel that's necessary.

Of course, if you'd rather, you can form a Link of Substitute Words for the French words. But since you probably won't be faced with this specific memory problem until you already know the French words and their meanings, that shouldn't be necessary. There are many ways to handle this problem, and as you continue reading you'll become aware of them, but the above (or a similar Link) will serve the purpose. Try it and see for yourself.

QUESTIONS AND ANSWERS:

QUESTION: Why does the Substitute Word system make it easier to memorize English and foreign vocabulary?

ANSWER: If you've tried the system on the examples I've given you, you already know the answer to this question. Applying the system forces you to pay attention; it forces you to be Originally Aware. It pinpoints your concentration by forcing you to follow the basic rule of memory; that is, by associating something new with something you already know (the meaning of a new word with the Substitute Word).

QUESTION: What if I can't come up with a word or phrase that sounds exactly like the word I want to remember?

ANSWER: Get as close as you can to the sound of the new word. Some foreign words may even have sounds that we don't have in English. It doesn't matter, get as close as possible. Remember, all you want or need is a *reminder;* it doesn't have to be exact. That's why I used *écureuil* as an example; there is no sound in the English language that's exactly like the French "euil" sound. Yet the Substitute Word system is still applicable; it will still enable you to learn the word easily.

QUESTION: Will the Substitute Word system help me remember any words in any language?

ANSWER: There is no limit to how many, or what kind of, words you can remember by applying the Substitute Word system of memory. If you didn't know the system, you'd have to remember foreign words by rote memory. You might as well make it easier for yourself and use my system. As you use the words you've memorized with the system, they'll become etched into your memory. The original associations will fade because you won't need them anymore.

QUESTION: What if I can't picture the meaning of a word I want to remember?

ANSWER: Simply make up a Substitute Word for both (the sound of the new word *and* its meaning) and associate one with the other. Example: the word "anchorite" means hermit. Let's assume that you didn't know that a hermit is someone who lives all alone. You could picture an *anchor* up on a *height* wearing a girl's (baseball) mitt (*her mitt*). See this anchor being all alone. That will help you to remember both words, and also the meaning.

QUESTION: What about tough languages like Chinese and Japanese?

ANSWER: It will always be more difficult to memorize Chinese or Japanese words, whether or not you use my system. However, applying my system cannot help but make it faster and easier to memorize foreign words, no matter what the language is.

QUESTION: Can I apply the same idea to foreign phrases?

ANSWER: Of course. The phrase *Comment allez-vous?* means "How are you?" in French. You might see yourself shaking hands with someone, or throwing your arms around him ("How are you?") and you're saying, *"Come on,"* as you take him into an *alley* to show him the *view* (*come on alley view—comment allez-vous?*). *Rien de grave* is a French idiomatic expression meaning "(It's) not serious." Any ridiculous association between *ran the grave* and *not serious* would remind you of both the phrase and its meaning. Of course, simply forming a Link of the Substitute Words for each word in the phrase—as I memorized the Greek word for ant hole—would serve the purpose.

QUESTION: What about the pronunciation of foreign words?

ANSWER: Don't worry about it. We have to assume that if you are studying a foreign language, you already know the basics, such as the alphabet and pronunciation. Therefore, you will remember the pronunciation when you use the memory system. Keep in mind that you select a Substitute Word in the first place because it reminds you of the pronunciation of the word you want to remember.

QUESTION: Can a substitute word be found for *any* word?

ANSWER: Neither I nor any of my students have been stumped yet. You can always come up with something (even a thought that you can't put into words) that will be close enough to any word to remind you of it. And don't lose sight of the fact that just thinking of the new word in order to think of a Substitute Word helps to impress it on your consciousness.

11

NAMES AND NUMBERS

Whether or not it is necessary for you to memorize all the Presidents of the United States, this chapter will show you how to do it, by number, in minutes. Certainly, this knowledge can't hurt you. At the same time, it will show you how to memorize names and numbers of any kind, at any time.

A person's name is usually just as tangible or meaningless as a word in a language you don't know. That is why most people have trouble remembering names. But now you can picture a person's name! It's simple. Treat it exactly as if it were a foreign word you wanted to remember. That's all. The only difference is that to remember the Presidents, you have to remember a position or number, instead of a definition or meaning.

All you have to do is associate the Substitute Word for the President's name with the Peg Word for the position number. You can do it in minutes, if you know the Peg Words from (in this case) 1 to 37. If you don't know them, go back to pages 48–49 and learn them now. If you don't do that, you'll never really know whether or not this system works.

I'll help you with the first eight Presidents; then I'll give you some suggestions for the others and you're on your own. The first President of the United States was George Washington. What would remind you of the name Washington? *Wash* or *washing*, of course. Either one is a good Substitute Word, and will remind you of the name. But how will you remember that Washington is number 1?

No problem, because now you have a way of picturing the 1. What is your Peg Word for 1? *Tie,* of course. All you have to do is to associate tie with wash or washing. Picture yourself washing your tie while you're wearing it, or see yourself wearing a washing machine instead of a tie. Select one, and see that picture.

John Adams was the second President. What can you use as a Substitute Word for Adams? Try to think of one yourself. *A dam* has meaning, or you might think of a *fig leaf*, since that's what Adam wore in the Garden of Eden. Or try *at 'im, atom,* or *Adam's apple.*

Now what's your Peg Word for 2? *Noah.* Associate that with the Substitute Word you are using to remind you of Adams. You might see a man with a long gray beard (my picture for Noah) and millions of people are rushing *at 'im.* Or you might see an *atom* bomb exploding in a long gray beard. See the picture you've selected.

The third President was Thomas Jefferson. What can you use to remind you of the name Jefferson? Perhaps a nickel, because Jefferson's picture is on it, or Mutt and *Jeff,* the comic-strip characters. Or, since your Peg Word for 3 is *Ma,* you can picture yourself asking your mother, *"D'ja have a son?"* That *sounds like* Jefferson. Use whatever you like. If you use a nickel, you can see your mother's picture on it, or you can picture your mother covered with nickels.

James Madison was the fourth President. *Mad at son* sounds like Madison, so does *medicine.* Or you can use *Madison* Avenue. You might see a gigantic loaf of *rye* (4) bread taking *medicine,* or see Madison Avenue paved with rye bread or inundated with rye whiskey.

The fifth President was James Monroe. The Peg Word for 5 is *law.* For Monroe, you might use *man row,* or the *Monroe* Doctrine, or Marilyn *Monroe.* If you saw Marilyn Monroe dressed as a policeman, walking the beat, that would do it. You might also picture a *man row*ing a policeman.

John Quincy Adams was the sixth President. Use whatever you used for Adams before, but now associate it with your

Peg Word for 6—*shoe*. Perhaps you're wearing *atom* bombs instead of shoes.

The seventh President was Andrew Jackson, and the Peg Word for 7 is *cow*. With cow, associate a *jack,* either the kind you lift a car with, or the kind little girls play with. You might see yourself milking a cow and millions of jacks come out instead of milk, or you could be lifting a cow with a jack.

Although it isn't necessary to get a reminder for *son* into your picture—*jack* is enough to remind you of Jackson—you can if you want to. I always see one of the objects smaller than the others. That always represents *son* to me; it's my standard for *son*.

Martin Van Buren was the eighth President, and the Peg Word for 8 is *ivy*. All you need is something to remind you of the name Van Buren. *Van* would do it, because no other President has that syllable in his name. You could also use *bureau* for Buren—or both. For example, you might picture yourself opening your *bureau* drawer and a moving *van* full of *ivy* comes out and hits you. Millions of vans growing on a wall instead of ivy would also do it.

If you've tried to make the associations, if you've seen the pictures for each one, there's no doubt that you now know them all. Try it; see if you know the Presidents from 1 to 8. When you've done that, try to fill in these blanks.

President number 6 was ...... President number 5 was ......
President number 1 was ...... President number 2 was ......
President number 4 was ...... President number 7 was ......
President number 8 was ...... President number 3 was ......

And these:

Jackson was number ....   Washington was number ....
Van Buren was number ....   Adams was number ....
                              (and number ....)
Madison was number ....

Do you see that it does work? It's easy. You can learn all the Presidents in just a short time. Do it on your own. Use the last names only; I'll discuss the first names later. Here are the other Presidents. I'll give you the Peg Word (although you should know them now) for each one, and also a suggestion for a Substitute Word. You make up the ridiculous pictures. If you really want to learn the Presidents, I'd suggest you do a few at a time. Stop to review (simply go over your associations mentally), then learn some more.

9. William Harrison ..... *bee* to *hairy* (or *hurry*) *son*.
10. John Tyler . .... *toes* to *tiler* (one who tiles).
11. James Polk .... *tot* to *poke*.
12. Zachary Taylor ...... *tin* to *tailor*.
13. Millard Fillmore .... *tomb* to *fill more; feel more*.
14. Franklin Pierce ... ... *tire* to *pierce*.
15. James Buchanan .... *towel* to *blue* (or *blew*) *cannon*.
16. Abraham Lincoln .... *dish* to *penny* or *link on*.
17. Andrew Johnson ... *tack* to *yawn* (and) *son* or *jaw* and *son*.
18. Ulysses S. Grant ..... . *dove* to *granite, grand,* or *grant*.
19. Rutherford B. Hayes . *tub* to *hay* or *haze*.
20. James Garfield .... *nose* to *cigar field* or *car field*.
21. Chester A. Arthur . *net* to *author* or *ah there*.
22. Grover Cleveland . *nun* to *cleave land* (or *leave*) *land*.
23. Benjamin Harrison . . *name* to *hairy* (or *hurry*) *son*.
24. Grover Cleveland . *nero* to *cleave* (or *leave*) *land*.
25. William McKinley ... . *nail* to *Mack in lea, Mack can lie*.
26. Theodore Roosevelt *notch* to *rose* or *rose felt*.
27. William Taft ... . *neck* to *daft, taffy,* or *raft*.
28. Woodrow Wilson .. ... *knife* to *will son* or *wills on*.
29. Warren Harding . *knob* to *hard ink* or *hardening*.
30. Calvin Coolidge *mouse* to *cool ledge* or *cool itch*.
31. Herbert Hoover . *mat* to Hoover vacuum cleaner, *who where,* or *hoof air*.
32. Franklin D. Roosevelt ... *moon* to *rose* or *rose felt*.
33. Harry S. Truman ...... *mummy* to *true* (or *threw*) *man*.
34. Dwight D. Eisenhower .. *mower* to *I send hour* (clock); *ice in hour*.
35. John F. Kennedy .. ... *mule* to *can of D's* or *Kennedy* airport.

36. Lyndon B. Johnson ...... *match* to *yawn* and *son* or *jaw* and *son*.
37. Richard Nixon .... *mug* to *nicks on* or *nick sun*.

Have you tried to form an association for each one? If you really have, number a piece of paper from 1 to 37 and try to list all the Presidents. Or do it mentally. Count to yourself from 1 to 37. As you think of each number, the Peg Word should come to mind, and the Peg Word will tell you the correct President. Take a few moments and try it.

Of course, now you also know them in and out of order, by number, as you did the first eight Presidents. Stop reading for a few minutes and test yourself; you'll be pleasantly surprised.

So, you see, you can remember names (of things and places as well as people) with numbers. Nothing to it once you understand the Substitute Word idea, and once you know the Peg Words and the phonetic alphabet.

Usually, the last name is enough; the assumption is that you already know the names. What my system does is give you the *reminders* you need. But if you don't know all the Presidents' first names, it's no problem. Simply make up a Substitute Word for the first name and stick it into your original association.

For example, if you saw a picture of a *mummy throw*ing a *man* to help you remember that Truman was the thirty-third President, you can also see that mummy or that man being very *hairy*. *Hairy* is enough to remind you of Harry. Later on, you'll learn how to picture letters of the alphabet so that you'll also be able to remember Truman's middle initial, *S*, but for the time being, just picture a gigantic letter *S*.

Polk's first name was James. Your picture might have been of yourself *pok*ing a *tot* (I'd see my finger going right through the tot, to help make it ridiculous). If you can also see yourself *aim*ing your finger, that could remind you of James—*aim*s, James.

For William, you might see a *yam* (sweet potato) writing its *will*—*will yam,* William. For Zachary, you could picture yourself *carry*ing something in a *sack*—*sack carry,* Zachary.

In other words, you make up a Substitute Word for the first name, just as you did for the last name, and get it into your picture. Try it; you'll see that it works extremely well.

After you have been applying the system for a while, you'll have standards for certain names. That is, after you think of *robber* for Robert, for instance, you'll always use robber as the Substitute Word (or thought) for that name. Use the same idea to help you remember the name of a President's wife, or the names of his children, or what have you.

Also, after some experience you'll need only partial reminders. For example, if you associate *ice* or *eyes* with *mower,* that would probably be enough to remind you that the thirty-fourth (mower) President was *Eis*enhower. If you wanted to be sure to remember his first name, you could get *white* (Dwight) into the picture (you're painting the ice or eyes white).

If you want to remember who was Vice President during any President's term of office, that's easy. Think up a Substitute Word for the name (last name only, or both names, if you wish) and put it into your original picture.

For instance, you might have pictured a *mouse* (30) on a *cool ledge* to tell you that Coolidge was the thirtieth President. If you get some *doors* into that picture (see the mouse, or mice, coming out of doors), it would remind you that the Vice President was (Charles G.) Dawes. If you saw those doors *char*red, or having *quarrels,* it would remind you of Dawes's first name, Charles.

If you originally used a boy (son) *yawn*ing as the Substitute Word (or thought) for Johnson (*yawn son*), your picture would have included some *match*es (36). Or perhaps a smaller match (to remind you of son) was doing the yawning. See that smaller match giving a camel an extra *hump, free* of charge. That should remind you that Humphrey was Johnson's Vice President. If you want a reminder of Humphrey's first name, picture the camel saying, *"You bet* (Hubert), I'll take it."

You can also remember any dates or anything else pertaining to the Presidents. I'll be discussing that throughout the book.

12

MEMORIZING COLORS

This short chapter pertains to a subject that you probably are not studying—unless you're studying electronics. I'm including it, however, for a specific reason. It's another use for the phonetic alphabet (Peg Words) and the Substitute Word system. It is necessary for you to be thoroughly familiar with these ideas—the fundamentals—before you get to the more important academic examples. It's like swinging two bats to make it easier to swing one. It will also help you to see how the systems can be manipulated to help solve any memory problem.

All resistors are rated in *ohms* and are marked with four colored bands. In order to find the value of a resistor you would read the colored bands from left to right, following this national color code:

brown—1	gray—8
red—2	white—9
orange—3	black—0
yellow—4	Tolerance; plus or minus:
green—5	gold—5%
blue—6	silver—10%
violet—7	

I don't think it's necessary to mention just how these colors are used or how you'd read them; you'll know that if you are studying the subject. What is important here is to see how easy it is to remember the color code.

Ordinarily, colors are difficult to memorize because they are intangible. But if you make up a standard picture to represent each color, a picture that is tangible, then the problem is solved. Any picture will do, as long as it is a definite thing that reminds you of the color. Here are some of the pictures, or standards, that I use:

To remind me of brown, I always see someone *drown*ing; for red, I picture a bull (a bull charges a red cloth). For orange, I see an orange; for yellow, a banana; for green, grass; for blue, the sky; for violet, a violet (the flower) or *violence;* for gray, a *ray gun*; for white, a white flag (of surrender); for black, black paint; for gold, a gold coin (or *old, cold*); for silver, the Lone Ranger's horse Silver, or Long John Silver.

Once you've decided on a picture for each color, it is simple to remember anything else with that color. It really is child's play now. Try it; see these pictures clearly: a *tie* (1) drowning; *Noah* fighting a bull; your *Ma* eating a gigantic orange; you're cutting open a loaf of *rye* bread and finding a banana inside; a policeman (*law*) arresting millions of blades of grass; the sky as one gigantic *shoe;* you're milking a *cow* and violets come out instead of milk; you're shooting *ivy* from a wall with your ray gun; a gigantic *bee* waving a white flag; you're painting your *toes* black (for number 10; or use *zoo* for zero); a gold coin climbing a hill (I don't use the basic Peg Word for 5 here so as not to confuse it with 5—green; I want to remember that gold means 5 *percent*); you're teasing (*tease*—10 percent) the Lone Ranger's horse.

See each of these ridiculous pictures once and you'll know the number that each color represents. Of course, if you were studying electronics you'd know that if a resistor has a blue, green, red, and silver band from left to right, its value is 6500 ohms, plus or minus 10%. Blue = 6, green = 5. The third band is called the multiplier; it tells you the number of zeros that follow the first two digits (red = 2; two zeros). Silver is 10% tolerance, plus or minus (the tolerance color band is always the last band).

There's another way to solve the above problem easily. I mention it now for completion's sake, and to show you how the systems can be manipulated. All you have to do is to start the word with the same letter (or letters where necessary) as the color, and to let the next consonant sound in the word tell you the number. Look:

*brat—br*own, 1 (two letters for brown because there are other colors here that begin with *B*)
run, or *rain—r*ed, 2
ohm, or *om*elet—*o*range, 3
*year—y*ellow, 4 (picture a calendar for year)
*grill—gr*een, 5
*blush—blu*e, 6 (three letters, blu, to differentiate from black)
Vicks, or *V*iking—*v*iolet, 7
*gravy—gra*y, 8 (*gra* to differentiate from *gr* for green)
*wipe—w*hite, 9 (or *whip* if you'd rather)
*blast—bla*ck, 0

Incidentally, I've given you the standards that I use for the colors in this example only. Obviously, if you have to remember other colors for any reason, make up a standard picture for each of them. For purple, you might think of a grape; for tan, a tam (beret).

It makes no difference what you use as long as that's what comes to mind when you think of the color. When I needed a standard for indigo, I pictured Frank Sinatra because a few days earlier I had heard Sinatra's recording of "Mood Indigo." When I thought of indigo, that's what came to mind. That was years ago, but I still use Sinatra as my standard for indigo. When I needed a word for beige, I thought of a beige carpet I had at home at the time. I no longer have the carpet, but a picture of a carpet still reminds me of beige.

The point is that once you've thought of a word to represent something and have used it once or twice, that same word will instantly come to mind when you think of the thing again. It's important that you understand this fact.

13

SPELLING

Talking to students and professors while researching this book made me realize that many students, even at higher levels of education, had some spelling problems. That's the reason for this chapter. You will be judged by the way you spell for the rest of your life, and I know that I, personally, would think twice before doing business with someone who used such spellings as "goverment," "lonly," "libary," and "sauser."

Actually, spelling is a memory problem; you have to remember letters, sounds, rules, exceptions to rules, and so on. To solve many spelling problems, you can use the basic memory rule which, as you know by now, is: Associate something you want to remember with something you already know or remember.

Do you realize that the more you know or remember, the more you can remember? It's true, because the more you know, the more you have at your command to associate with new things. That is why you can never remember too much.

The systems in this book are meant to be aids only; they are not intended to be the only way to learn to spell properly. What I've tried to do is show you how to see things with your mind. You should apply this idea to spelling. A good speller first sees the word he wants to spell in his mind; then he writes or spells what he sees there.

All the words used in this chapter as examples are words that high school students have misspelled on exams. When I was going to school I always misspelled the word "rhythm." I finally solved the problem by forming a ridiculous picture in my mind of a two-headed monster playing "red hot" rhythm.

The phrase I thought of whenever I thought of the word was, "*red hot, you two-headed monster.*"

Silly, of course—but it worked! The problem is that if you did that with all the words you habitually misspelled, it would get confusing. There are better ways to get rid of habitual spelling errors.

Most spelling errors *are* habitual. That is, we make the same error consistently. The problem usually is that we don't think at the moment we make that error. It's easier to do what we've always done.

You can solve the problem by bringing the error into your conscious mind—that is, by *forcing* yourself to think about it.

Many people misspell the word "calendar"; it is often spelled calend*e*r. Assuming you make the same mistake, here's how to solve it. Print the word on a piece of paper, spelled the *wrong* way. Print the incorrect letter larger than the others: calend E r. Then put an *X* (to show that it is wrong) through the wrong letter: calend ✗ r. Do that *five* times. I know it sounds silly—but *do* it.

This action has made you aware of the error, because you have now made the error consciously. Now print the word correctly; make the correct letter larger than the others: calend A r. Underline or circle the correct letter: calend Ⓐ r. Do that *five* times.

If you do it exactly like that, I guarantee you'll never again misspell calendar. Printing it the wrong way five times has made you conscious of the habitual error. Printing it correctly five times has "locked in" the correct spelling. You've taken the first step toward making the correct spelling habitual!

Another common spelling error is the word "separate"; it is often misspelled: sep*e*rate. Solve the problem by doing the same thing you did before. Five times: sep ✗ rate; and five times: sep Ⓐ rate.

You have to find the words that habitually cause you

trouble and then apply this idea. Here are some that you might want to try:

ar*c*tic—not artic.	pro*f*essor—not proffessor.
ta*ri*ff—not tarriff.	fortunate*ly*—not fortunatly.
e*s*capade—not excapade.	ex*h*ibition—not exibition.
mor*t*gage—not morgage.	recei*p*t—not receit.
bi*c*ycle—not bicicle.	ac*tor*—not acter.
lon*e*ly—not lonly.	mi*s*spell—not mispell.
je*we*lry—not jewlry.	bound*a*ry—not boundery.
	mu*s*cle—not musle, or mussle.

Association will also help you to solve many spelling problems. There are a few different ways to handle it.

I once had an adult student who told me that he always confused the names Au*b*rey and Au*d*rey; he always forgot which was male (Aubrey) and which was female (Audrey). The problem was easily solved when I told him to think of it this way: the *B* in Au*b*rey would stand for *boy;* the *D* in Au*d*rey would stand for *d*oll or *d*ame.

The name Franc*es* is female; Franc*is* is male. Do you want to be sure of the correct spelling? Easy; think of this: Franc*es* —h*er* (or sh*e*); Franc*is*—h*im* (or h*is*). Actually, you don't need both of them; just associating Franc*is* to h*is* will take care of both.

A common error is to mix up the spelling and meaning of the words station*e*ry and station*a*ry. Station*e*ry refers to writing material such as paper and envelopes. Station*a*ry means standing still. Look at this:

station *e* ry—writ *e* (you also use station*ery* to write a lett*er*)
station *a* ry—st *a* nd

Concentrate on that for a moment or two, and stationery and stationary will never cause you trouble again! A princip*le* is a rule; a princip*al* is the first or highest, like the principal of your school. The difference in spelling and meaning is easy to remember. Concentrate on this:

> (a) princip *le*–is a ru *le*
> (your) princi *pal*–is your *pal*

Capit*o*l is spelled with an *O* when it refers to the building in Washington, D.C., or any building where the legislature of a state or country sits. Capit*a*l with an *A* is the spelling for the capital city of a state or country, or for the word that means money.

capit *a* l–*c a* sh (or the *first* city of a state, *a* is the *first* letter)
capit *o* l–d *o* me

Presen*c*e is the opposite of absen*c*e; present*s* are gift*s*.
You *eat* a st*eak*, not a *stake*.
A sove*reign reign*s; it r*ain*s w*ater*.
The h*eat* causes bad w*eat*her, not *whether*.
A coun*ci*l s*i*ts; a coun*se*l advi*se*s.

You can apply this idea to words that sound different but are spelled so much alike that they cause confusion—like *desert* and *dessert*.

> de*s*ert–*s*and (one *S*)
> de*ss*ert–is eaten after di*nn*er (double letter)

Many words that cause trouble contain smaller words that you already know. An association between the two would solve the problem. I mentioned one such association at the beginning of the book: Never be*lie*ve a *lie*. If you have trouble with the word piece, think of this: have a *pie*ce of *pie*. Or if the war will c*ease* we'll have p*eace*.

Does the word "colossal" cause you trouble? Is it a double *L* or a double *S*? Picture this in your mind: you suffered a co*loss*al *loss*. Here are a few more examples of this idea. And

it will also help if you form a ridiculous picture in your mind
for each one that has ever caused you trouble.

Picture a gigantic number 9 (*nine*) wearing a dress; it's
fem*inine*.

You're g*rate*ful that you *ate*. (P*ardon* the gramm*ar*—not
gramm*er*!)

Iron is part of the envi*ron*ment.

You made a *gain* by getting a bar*gain*.

You have an ar*gum*ent over some *gum*.

A *guard* *guar*antees safety.

You told your *secret*ary a *secret*.

You *err* when you inte*rr*upt.

A cat*alog* advertised *a log* for sale.

See *all* lines being par*all*el.

To *age* is no tr*age*dy.

See if you can make up pictures for these:

kindergar*ten*	*bus*iness	ne*cess*ary
mis*chief*	*peas*ant	*court*esy
deter*mine*	fr*eight*	per*man*ent
*labor*atory	*ill*ustrate	capa*city*

Just because a troublesome word does not contain a word
you already know doesn't mean that you can't use association.
Some people have trouble spelling *occasion* correctly; is it a
double *C* or a double *S*? If you already know how to spell the
word *accident,* this association—on o*cc*asion I have an a*cc*i-
dent—will remind you that o*cc*asion is spelled with a double
C.

"Alright" is incorrect; "all right" is correct. Just think of
all right being the opposite of *all wrong.*

If you put a *D* in the middle of "with," it gives the word
more *width.*

The *GM* company used good jud*gm*ent in making cars.

It's so *dark* I can't see my calen*dar.* You could also see
yourself throwing *dart*s at your calendar.

There's a lone *E* in lonely.
You usually put a *c*up on a sau*c*er.

It doesn't matter how silly or crazy any association is. The sillier it is, the better it is. Thinking up associations is also good exercise for the imagination and encourages creativity.

A student once told me that he had trouble spelling the word "motorcycle"; he habitually spelled it with an *e*—motercycle. I solved the problem by drawing this on the blackboard: MⱭTⱭRCYCLE. You are limited only by your own imagination!

There is only one word in the English language that has the "sede" ending. That's the word "supersede." You can use the printing-five-times method suggested earlier to help you remember it, or you can see a picture in your mind of a gigantic *super seed*, the kind you plant. That'll remind you of the *S*.

There are quite a few "cede" endings, but only three "ceed" endings. If you want to remember the latter three, think of this sentence or, more important, try to picture it: "In order to suc*ceed* you have to pro*ceed* to ex*ceed*."

I guess the best-known spelling rule is:

> *I* before *E*,
> Except after *C*;
> Or when sounded as *A*,
> As in n*ei*ghbor and w*ei*gh.

However, there are many exceptions to the rule, such as counterf*ei*t, prot*ei*n, caff*ei*ne, sh*ei*k, cod*ei*ne. These and some other common exceptions can be remembered by thinking of these sentences: "The counterf*ei*t sh*ei*k thought that caff*ei*ne and cod*ei*ne gave him prot*ei*n" and "The w*ei*rd financ*ie*r s*ei*zes n*ei*ther l*ei*sure nor pleasure."

Elsewhere in this book we will be discussing the letters of

the alphabet. You'll be able to use the method of picturing them to help you with the spelling of other troublesome words.

You can solve any spelling problem by applying these ideas. As I mentioned at the start of this section, the memory aids by themselves won't make you a good speller, but when used in conjunction with your basic knowledge of letters, sounds, and rules, they cannot help but make you a better speller. In addition, searching for an association for any word forces you to concentrate on that word as you never have before.

14

THE CLASSICS

A good exercise for both the Substitute Word idea and the Link system would be to memorize the twenty-seven works of Plato. Here is the list of Plato's works, in alphabetical order:

Alcibiades	Hippias Minor	Phaedrus
Apology	Ion	Philebus
Charmides	Laches	Politicus
Cratylus	Laws	Protagoras
Critias	Letters	Republic
Crito	Lysis	Sophist
Euthydemus	Meno	Symposium
Euthyphro	Parmenides	Theaetetus
Gorgias	Phaedo	Timaeus

Let's try it. Please bear in mind that the Substitute Words I suggest are the ones that come to my mind. Therefore, they're the ones that would remind me of the titles. You'd be better off using the ones you think of. Be sure to concentrate on the pictures.

Al sees a bee in *Hades* (Alcibiades) and *apologizes* to it (Apology).

Some *charming D's* or *charmer dies* (Charmides) are apologizing to you.

The charming D's fly into a *crate* that's being carried by an *ill ass* (Cratylus).

This crate (on the ill ass) falls into a *creek* full of *teas,* or the crate is the *grittiest* (Critias); *gritty ass* (donkey) would also do.

A *toe* falls into the creek and *cries* (Crito).

The toe turns into a *youth* who is *muss*ing up *a dame* (Euthydemus).

The dame makes the *youth* sway to and *fro* (Euthyphro).

The youth looks *gorgeous* (Gorgias) as he sways to and fro.

A *hippie miner* (Hippias Minor) throws coal at the gorgeous youth; or a hippie miner is gorgeous.

The hippie miner digs for *iron* (Ion).

The iron is thrown into a *lake* and turns into millions of *keys* (Laches).

The *law* (Law) comes to arrest all the keys.

The law writes *letters* (Letters) to the keys' parents.

A gigantic letter throws *lye* at its *sis*ter (Lysis).

The sister screams, "Me? No!" (Meno); or a *mean O* throws lye at her.

A mean *O* is playing golf with the good golfers, the *par men,* who *are* all *D's* (Parmenides).

The *D's fade* (Phaedo) as they play golf.

As a *D fades* it holds a *rose,* which fades with it (Phaedrus).

You *fill a bus* (Philebus) with faded roses.

A bus is filled with *politicians* (Politicus).

The politicians send a *pro to gore us* (Protagoras).

The pro gores everyone, the entire *public,* and/or does it publicly (Republic).

The public *sews* the pro's *fist* (Sophist).

Lots of fists are holding a *symposium* (Symposium).

Everybody at the symposium eats 'taters—*they eat 'taters* (Theaetetus).

People are having a race eating 'taters, and they ask you to *"Time us"* (Timaeus).

If you form this Link, see each picture clearly and review them a few times. Then you'll have a reminder for each title in Plato's works. I'd suggest that you start the Link with a Substitute Word for Plato, so you'll know what it is you're remembering.

Although it would probably never be necessary to know these titles by number, you might like to use the Peg system; it will work just as well. Associate tie (1) with *Al sees a bee in Hades,* and Noah (2) with *apology,* Ma (3) with *charming D's,* and continue on to neck (27) for *time us.*

You may not find it necessary to remember all of Plato's works, but it is well to understand the idea so that you can apply it to similar things that you may have to, or want to, remember. For example, in the study of the classics, you may want to memorize some of the names of people and places.

If you wanted to remember that Penthesilea was the queen of the Amazons, you might see a ridiculous picture of gigantic women (Amazons) wearing *pants* and acting *silly.* Associating Amazons to *penicillin* would do as well.

Bacchus is the god of wine. Picture millions of bottles, or barrels, of wine on the *back* of an *ass.*

Circe is a goddess whose name means "hawk." I originally remembered this piece of information by picturing myself pointing out a hawk to a gentleman, *"Sir, see the hawk."*

Imagine a gigantic *vest* (Vesta) keeping a fire burning in a *hearth.* Vesta is the goddess of the sacred hearth fire.

Cambyses was a Persian king who added Egypt to the empire. Picture a king, wearing a Persian rug instead of a cape, with his army *camp*ed *by seas,* bringing a pyramid (Egypt) to his country.

See many *E's* and *O's* being *heal*ed (Helios) by flying into the sun to remind you that Helios is the goddess of the sun. Or you can see *helium* coming out of the sun.

Picture yourself remembering the name of every sign (*name o' sign*—Mnemosyne) and you'll remember that Mnemosyne is the goddess of memory.

Picture a gigantic *iris* (the flower) running back and forth between the gods, delivering messages. Iris was the female messenger of the gods.

Ausonia was another name for Italy. See a boot (Italy), or *a tall E,* talking to a girl named Sonia; it is saying, *"Aw, Sonia."*

Eurotas is the name of a river in Greece. Picture someone writing to you *(you wrote us)* from a river full of *grease.* If you want to, you can picture yourself receiving only *part* of the letter, to remind you that the river is in Sparta.

This simple application of the Substitute Word system can be used to help you learn the terminology of any subject; I've used examples of this throughout the book. Would you like to test yourself on what you've read in this chapter? Go over the examples and then answer these questions:

List Plato's twenty-seven works: . . . .
. . . .
. . . .
. . . .
. . . .

Who or what are the following:

Iris	Mnemosyne . . . .
Penthesilea	Eurotas . . . .
Circe	Helios . . . .
Vesta	Ausonia . . . .
Cambyses	Bacchus . . . .

If you want some more practice, try learning the works of Ovid. You might start a Link with, say, *overhead* or *O wed.* Associate that with *ah more rays* or lovers (Amores) with *hero dies* (Heroides) with *R's tearing a mat* (Ars Amatoria) with *media* (or *remedial* or *meat ear*) *amore* (Remedia Amoris) with *medicine face* (Medicina Faciei) with *my dear* or *meatier* (Medea) with *met more posies* (Metamorphoses) with *fast* or *fast tea* (Fasti) with *twist ear* (Tristia) with *a pistol lay*ing *eggs* that someone *punts* with his *toe* (Epistulae

Ex Ponto) with *hale E Utica* or *you tick her* (Halieutica) with *eye bus* (Ibis).

Form your own silly pictures and see how quickly you can memorize these titles. If you want to remember that **Ovid was** born in 43 B.C. and died in A.D. 18, picture a ram (43) charging a dove (18) that flies *overhead*.

15

MEMORIZING DATES AND EVENTS

Some students tell me that it is no longer necessary to remember specific dates; others tell me that although it may not be necessary, it can be a plus to do so; still others tell me that their teachers insist that they remember them. In many cases it is the sequence of events that has to be remembered, not especially the dates themselves. However, I can't think of a better way to establish a sequence of events than to remember the dates.

I don't know whether it would be useful for you to remember the years in which certain states were admitted to the Union. Perhaps it would be useful only if certain significant events occurred in history at about the same time. Fine. Associate the significant event with the state and the date. I'll leave that to you. Meanwhile, we'll see how easy it is to memorize the states and the dates of their admission to the Union.

Simply associate a Substitute Word for the state name with the date. You probably won't have to bother with the century digits, because most of the dates are either in the late 1700's or in the 1800's. All you really have to get into your picture is a word to remind you of the year. For that you can use your basic Peg Words or any words that fit phonetically. I'll give you suggestions for the Substitute Words and digit words; you form your own pictures.

Vermont was admitted to the Union in 1791. A picture of *vermin* filling a gigantic *pot* will do the trick. If you want the entire date, *took pot* will do.

Kentucky was admitted in 1792. You *can't talk* because there's a *dog bone* in your throat—or just *bone* for 92.

97

Tennessee—1796. Associate *ten, I see* or *tennis see* with *badge* or *duck bush*.

Ohio—1803. Associate *hi* or *high O* with *sum* or *seam*.

Louisiana—1812. Associate *loose, Louise,* or *lose Anna* with *tin*.

Indiana—1816. Associate *Indian* with *dish*.

Mississippi—1817. Associate *sip* or *Mrs. sip* with *tack*.

Illinois—1818. A picture of a *dove* that's *ill* will do it.

Alabama—1819. Associate *album* with *tub*.

Maine—1820. Associate water *main* with *nose*—or *divans* for the entire date, or just *vans*, since you know that the first digit is a 1.

Michigan—1837. Associate *mix again* with *mug*.

Texas and Florida—1845. Associate *taxes* or *taxis* and *flower there* with *rail* or *roll*.

Iowa—1846. Associate *I owe her* with *roach* or *rash*.

Minnesota—1858. Associate *mini soda* with *leaf* or *love*.

Nevada—1864. Associate *never there* (or gambling) with *chair* or *jar*.

Colorado—1876. Associate *color a toe* (or just *color* or *collar*) with *cash* or *cage*.

Obviously, you can put any information you like into each association, and you will certainly find it works faster and is less of a chore than using rote memory. You won't realize that, however, if you have only read what I've written. For it to work you must actually *do* what I suggest.

In an earlier chapter I showed you how to remember all the Presidents by number or position. I said then that you could remember any dates connected with them at the same time. President Grant, for example, was born in 1822. Since you most likely already know the century, all you need is something to remind you of 22. A ridiculous picture associating *granite* (Grant) with nun (22) would do it.

James Madison (the fourth President) was born in 1751

and died in 1836. Simply associate your Substitute Word for Madison with *lot match* or *let 'im chew* (or *itch*). Again, you probably know the century. If you don't, simply use the words or phrases that make up the dates (*tickled*—1751; *tough match*—1836).

It's rarely necessary in your studies for you to learn the day and month of a historical event, but you can if you want to. Since there are twelve months in the year, the word or phrase you use should begin with the consonant sound that represents the number for that month. The next sound can tell you the day (1 to 31), and the next one the year. You can form a word or phrase to tell you anything you want it to tell you.

If you want to remember that Neil Armstrong was the first man to step onto the moon, and that it happened in 1969, picture a man with a very *strong arm* (Armstrong) stepping from a *ship* (69) onto the moon. If you want to remember the day and month of this historic event, you can see the man stepping on millions of *cans* (720—seventh month, twentieth day). For the month and year only, you could have used *ketchup* (769—seventh month, 1969).

There are other ways, of course. You could make up a word or thought to represent the name of each month, and get that into your picture whenever you need it. For example, a *maypole* could always represent May; firecrackers or a *jewel* could always represent July. A *gust* of wind could represent August; *janitor*, January; *ape* or showers, April; and so on.

Using President Grant as an example again—he was born on April 27, 1822, and inaugurated President in 1869. A gigantic piece of *granite* is putting a *ring* (427—April 27) on a *nun's* (22) finger. If you want to remember the year of his inauguration, get *ship, chip, chop,* or *shop* into your picture. If you want to have a reminder of the century, just put it in; *deafenin'* would give you the entire year.

For President Madison, *meat chilled* or *me touch lad*

(3–16–'51) would give you the entire birthdate; *showin' off much* (6–28–'36) is the date of his death. For any of these examples, you'd put the pictures for dates and other information into your original association. Your original association for Madison might have been of a gigantic loaf of rye (4) bread taking *medicine* (Madison). If, at the same time, you pictured the rye laughing because it was being *tickled* by a *tough match*, you'd be reminded of the dates of his birth and death.

Rutherford Hayes was born in Ohio. Your original association might have been of a tub (19) full of *hay*. If you want to remember that Hayes was born in Ohio, see the tub full of hay seeing an old friend and saying, "Oh, hi." If you pictured the hay saying that to a *nun,* it would remind you that Hayes was born in 1822.

William Taft's term of office was 19*09* to 19*13*. Just get *sub team* or *soaped* hi*m* into your original association.

Let's assume that you want to memorize the historical events listed below. Try to memorize them, using my suggestions or your own ideas, but always remember that you are better off forming your own Substitute Words and associations. A test will follow just to show you how well you have done.

William Shakespeare was born on April 26, 1564.

You're on a *ranch* (426—April 26), *shak*ing a *spear* in a *tall jar* (1564). If all you wanted to remember was the month and year, *rattle chair* or *rattle jar* (4–1564) would do it.

Benjamin Franklin flew his famous kite on June 15, 1752.

See a gigantic *frank*furter (Franklin) on a *sh*uttle (or *show tell*) (615—June 15), flying a kite that he is *ticklin'* (1752). If you already know that this took place in the 1700's, a word for 52 (*lion*) would be all you'd need.

The first message over the first telegraph line was on May 24, 1844.

See a telegraph wire rowing (*rower*—44) to the moon; it's making a *lunar* (524—May 24) trip. You should know that this couldn't have happened in 1744 or 1944.

Alaska was purchased from Russia on March 30, 1867.

You're purchasing a baked *Alaska* (or *I'll ask her, last car*), which is filled with *mums* (330—March 30), with a gigantic *check* (67).

Custer's Last Stand occurred on June 25, 1876.

See lots of *custar*d (Custer; or *cussed her*) crossing the *channel* (625—June 25), carrying lots of *cash* (76).

Lincoln delivered his Gettysburg Address on November 19, 1863.

You might see a gigantic (Lincoln) penny *getting his burg*er (Gettysburg), which is all *tied* with *tape* (1119—November 19) and which he spreads with *jam* (63).

Go over all your associations, review all the information, and then fill in the dates (day, month, year) for all these events:

President Grant was born on . . . .; he was inaugurated in 18 . . . .
Custer's Last Stand took place on . . . .
William Shakespeare was born on . . . .
Lincoln gave his Gettysburg Address on . . . .

Benjamin Franklin flew his kite on ....
Alaska was purchased from Russia on ....
The first message over the first telegraph line was on ....

Here are some more historical facts with which to test your new amazing memory power:

In 1519, Magellan of Spain sailed his ship around the world. *Tilt up* or *tall top* would transpose to 1519; a tall top is *mad* and *yellin'* (Magellan) because it's in *pain* (Spain); the pain is being caused by a ship sailing all around it. I've put all the facts into the picture, but obviously, you need put in only what you feel you want to be reminded of.

In 1961, Gagarin of Russia went around the earth in space. A gigantic *sheet* (61) is being used as a *gag,* but some *air* gets *in* (*gag air in*—Gagarin); the person with the gag *rushes* (Russia) into *space* and goes *around the earth.*

All the following events took place in the 1800's, so all you'd need in your association would be a word to represent the last two digits. Washington, D.C., became the capital of the United States in 1800. Your *sis* (00) is *washing* (Washington) the dome of a capitol building.

The Louisiana Territory was purchased from France in 1803. A large *sum* (03) is paid to some *ants* (France) for *Louise.*

In 1807, Robert Fulton sailed his steamboat, the *Clermont.* A steamboat comes out of a *sack* (07) and—if you want to remember the steamboat's name—goes *clear* up a *mount*ain (Clermont).

The Texans fought the Mexicans at the Alamo in 1836. *Match*es (36) are fighting Mexicans (men wearing sombreros, perhaps) and perhaps they're *all* named *Moe.*

For dates you can use the basic Peg Words or, if you wish, other words. It doesn't matter which you use, as long as a word fits the association and fits phonetically. For example, a question on a history exam asked the student to name the

Republican candidates for President in 1932, 1936, and 1940. The answers are: Hoover, Landon, and Willkie. Form the following associations and you'll never forget these dates and names: you're cleaning the *moon* (32) with a *Hoover* vacuum cleaner; you *land on* a gigantic lighted *match* (36); a *rose* (40) *wilts* and becomes a *key.*

As I mentioned before, it is probably more important to remember the sequence of historical events than the dates. That's easy enough; simply Link the events. Now, however, you also have some varied examples of dates and events, so that you'll know how to remember them if you have to, or want to. There are more examples in the next chapter and throughout the book. The fact is that all the examples I've used have been and are still being used on exams.

You may also find it worthwhile to remember what caused certain events and what the results were. The Lincoln-Douglas debates took place in 1858. Lincoln lost that particular election, but the debates built his reputation and probably led to his victory in the next presidential election.

If you want to remember all that, associate Lincoln and Douglas with the date; perhaps a gigantic Lincoln penny is digging glass (*dig,* or *dug, glass*—Douglas) out of *tough lava* (1858). Or the penny is digging the glass with a *tough leaf.* That will remind you of the event and the date. Now include anything that will remind you of the result. Perhaps the Lincoln penny is growing or building something with the glass (his reputation grew, or was built); the penny grows into a white house (helped him become President).

I'm using all these different examples mainly to show you that you can put whatever you want to into your associations.

Every once in a while you'll find an almost logical and obvious association to help you remember a particular piece of information. For example, President *Van* Buren was born in 1782. Van tells you both his name and the last two digits of the year.

Abraham Lincoln was born in 1809. His nickname, A*be*, transposes to 9, which would help you remember the year. Benjamin Franklin was born in 1706; he was considered a *sage*. Napoleon was crowned emperor in 1804; picture the crown being so heavy it made his head *sore*. Lincoln was assassinated in 1865; see the perpetrators being pushed into *jail*. If you picture the *Titanic* sinking because it's made of *tin*, it will help you remember the date—1912.

This one has nothing to do with dates but, just by coincidence, the last three letters of Abra*ham Lin*coln's first name and the first three letters of his last name give you the name of his first-term Vice President, *Hamlin*.

Don't take the time to search for things like that, but if you happen to spot them, fine. Also, be sure to make them ridiculous; some of the above are not. I've mentioned them only because they're interesting; generally speaking, you'd be better off applying the systems as we have been doing.

And if you're thinking that it seems like a lot of work to apply the systems, you're making a big mistake. You're forgetting how much work it takes to memorize such information without any system!

The memory systems give you immediate reminders. Just thinking up Substitute Words and ridiculous pictures makes you concentrate on the material in such a way that it's already half learned.

Besides, in these examples I've included more information than is usually necessary. What you already know you can omit.

Once you start applying and using the systems, you'll do it faster and faster. Then I think you'll see how helpful they can be.

16

ALPHABET PEG WORDS

Most people don't really know their ABC's. Can you recite the alphabet backward? Can you instantly name the twelfth letter? The twenty-first? The eighteenth?

Letters are as difficult to remember as numbers because they are merely designs and do not readily create pictures in your mind. Nevertheless, it is possible to picture them. The idea is so simple you can learn it in a few minutes, and since it can be important for you to remember letters, I'd suggest you spend the necessary few minutes.

All you have to do is to decide on a word that sounds like each letter, and picture that for the letter from now on! For *A*, I always picture an *ape;* for *B*, I picture a *bean* (I don't use *bee* because that's my basic Peg Word for 9); for *C*, I picture the *sea*; for *D*, a college *dean*, and so on. Here's the entire list:

(tie)	A–ape	(tire)	N–hen
(Noah)	B–bean	(towel)	O–old (or eau–water)
(Ma)	C–sea	(dish)	P–pea
(rye)	D–dean	(tack)	Q–cue (stick)
(law)	E–eel	(dove)	R–art (or hour–clock)
(shoe)	F–half (or *eff*ort)	(tub)	S–ess curve
(cow)	G–jeans	(nose)	T–tea
(ivy)	H–age, itch (or ache)	(net)	U–ewe (or youth)
(bee)	I–eye	(nun)	V–veal (or victory)
(toes)	J–jail (or jay bird)	(name)	W–Waterloo
(tot)	K–cake (or cane)	(Nero)	X–eggs (or exit)
(tin)	L–el (elevated train)	(nail)	Y–wine
(tomb)	M–ham, hem (or *em*peror)	(notch)	Z–zebra

You can change any word you like; just be sure that the words you use can be *pictured* and sound like the letters.

If you use *hour* for R, picture a clock; for *Waterloo* I always picture Napoleon; you can use *trouble you* if you'd rather and picture yourself getting into trouble.

Just go over these words a few times, and you'll know them. Now, whenever you have to remember a letter, simply put the word that represents the letter into your picture or association. It will come in handy when you want to remember formulas or symbols of any kind, as you will see.

The fact that you can picture a letter also serves as a weapon for fighting spelling errors. If you have trouble remembering whether the word is spelled insur*a*nce or insur*e*nce, picture an *ape* selling insur*a*nce. That will tell you the word is spelled with an *A*. If you make an association of an *eel* having a pleasant exist*e*nce, it will remind you that this word is spelled with an *E*. Picture *two hams* shooting amm*u*nition at each other; an *ape* receiving an allow*a*nce, or an *eel* performing surg*e*ry.

Another reason for learning the alphabet this way is so it can be used as an alternate Peg list. That's why I placed the basic Peg Words in front of each one. Do you see? If you associate *tie* with *ape,* you'll know that *A* is the *first* letter (because *ape* represents *A* and *tie* represents 1).

Associate *tomb* with *ham* or *hem* and you'll know that *M* is the thirteenth letter; picture a *tub* going around an *ess curve* and you'll always know that *S* is the nineteenth letter of the alphabet. If you make a ridiculous association for each letter (down to a large *notch* in a *zebra*) you'll know all their numerical positions.

Once you know the positions, they can act as a Peg list because now each letter will represent a number in your mind just as your basic Peg Words do. In other words, whatever you associate with, say, a *hen,* would be number 14. This extra Peg list has a variety of uses.

One obvious use is to remember two lists, by number, at the same time. Although you could do it using only the basic

Peg Words, you might want to use the alphabet Pegs for the second list. Another, and more important, use would be when you're trying to memorize something with, say, more than one 4 in it, like a formula. Then you could use *rye* to represent one 4 and, to avoid confusion, *dean* to represent another 4.

There are many ways to form Peg lists. The phonetic alphabet is still the best way, but the alphabet Peg list is good for emergencies, even though it goes up only to 26. The first Peg list I ever used was one that went up to 10. It came from the "Children's Marching Song," a song we sang as children.

It started, "This old man, number one, he played knick-knack on a gun. . . ." The words I used were based on that song; they rhymed with the numbers. Look:

1. gun	6. sticks
2. glue	7. heaven
3. tree	8. gate
4. door	9. vine
5. hive	10. pen

The original word for 2 was shoe, but that would conflict with the phonetic Peg Word for 6. It really doesn't matter, though, because you'll know which Peg list you're using and therefore will know which number the word represents.

The above works exactly like your regular Peg-list words. It is, of course, limited to 10—although there are ways to expand it—but it can come in handy in emergencies when you need another word to represent a small number.

17

MORE DATES AND EVENTS

I've been told that it would be a great help, in the study of world history, to remember the kings and prime ministers of England. Here are the kings of England, and their dates of reign, from 1760 to the present:

George III; 1760–1820
George IV; 1820–1830
William IV; 1830–1837
Victoria; 1837–1901
Edward VII; 1901–1910
George V; 1910–1936
Edward VIII; 1936
George VI; 1936–1952
Elizabeth II; 1952–

If you need the sequence only, then you'd simply Link the names, or use the Peg Words from 1 to 9 (tie to bee). Of course, you can also use one of the alternate Peg lists—gun, glue, tree; or ape, bean, sea.

You have a choice of methods if you want to remember the dates. You can use a word to remind you of the last two digits of the year, if that's all you need; or you can use a word for the last three digits only, since you know that all the dates begin with a 1. For example, *catches* transposes to 760, but you'd know that it meant 1760.

Catches nose could represent the years of reign for George III. Catches is 1760 and nose is 20, which could mean only 1820. Another way to do it, if you know you're starting in 1760, is to put a word into your association that tells you the number of years in the reign. George III reigned for 60 years, so get *che*ese into the picture. Simple arithmetic will then give you the exact dates.

Assume you want to know the kings in order and their dates. Also assume that all you need are the last two digits and that you want to use the "Children's Marching Song" words. Very quickly then:

1 (gun). Picture a *gorge* with your *Ma* in it (George III); your Ma has a *gun* (using Ma cannot confuse you into thinking that this is the third item, since you know that you're using gun, glue, etc., for position). The gun shoots *che*ese (60) into her *no*se (20). This picture tells you that the first listing (gun) is George III (gorge Ma) and that he reigned from 1760 to 1820 (cheese nose). Be sure to see the picture clearly and you'll know the information.

2 (glue). George IV; 1820–1830. A gigantic loaf of *rye* bread is in a *gorge* (George IV). Associate this with *glue*, and that with, say, *no sums* (20–30).

3 (tree). William IV; 1830–1837. A *yam* is writing its *will* on a bottle of *rye* (William IV). Associate that with *tree*, and that with *messy mug* (30–37).

4 (door). Victoria; 1837–1901. A *door* is making the *victory* sign (Victoria). Associate that with *my gue*st or *make suit* (37–01).

5 (hive). Edward VII; 1901–1910. *A hive* of bees is attacking a hospital *ward* that has a *cow* in it (Edward VII). Associate that with, perhaps, a*cid hea*ds or *sit* (on) *toes* (01–10). Incidentally, if you feel that hive will conflict with your basic Peg Word for 9 (bee), use only the hive in your picture, not the insect. Or, if you like, you can change the word to *jive* or *live*.

6 (sticks). George V; 1910–1936. Some *sticks* are in a *gorge* and a policeman (*law*, 5) arrests them (George V). Associate that with *toss my sho*e, *this much*, *ties match* (10–36).

7 (heaven). Edward VIII; 1936. Picture a hospital *ward* full of *ivy* (Edward VIII) up in *heaven*. Associate that with *match* (36) or *tub match* (1936).

8 (gate). George VI; 1936–1952. A gigantic *shoe* is in a *gorge* (George VI); the shoe has a gigantic *gate* in it. Associate that with *my jawline, match lion, me shellin'*, or *Magellan* (36–52).

9 (vine). Elizabeth II; 1952–   Someone *lays a bed* (Elizabeth) onto a *vine; Noah* (2) or a man with a long gray beard (2, II) is sleeping in it. Associate that with *line, lion,* or *loan* (52).

Once you've formed the associations—really visualized the pictures—you'll have learned the material. Why don't you try it and then test yourself? You'll see how easy it is. If you wanted to learn the prime ministers of England, you'd form the same sort of Peg list.

I've used *gorge* as the Substitute Word for George; that's as good as any but, obviously, you can use any word you like. You can use *jaws, gorgeous,* or *gorge,* as in to gorge yourself with food. For Edward, you might have thought of *bed ward.* The ideas that come to you first are usually the best ones for you to use.

In tenth- or eleventh-grade social studies, it might be necessary for you to know the major Romanov rulers of Russia. It's easy enough to remember their names and the years of their reigns. You have the same choices here as you did with the British kings. Handle the dates the way that's best for you.

> Michael; 1613–1645
> Alexis; 1645–1676
> Peter I (the Great); 1689–1725
> Catherine II (the Great); 1762–1796
> Paul I; 1796–1801
> Alexander I; 1801–1825

Nicholas I; 1825–1855
Alexander II; 1855–1881
Alexander III; 1881–1894
Nicholas II; 1894–1917

For example: 613–45 would tell you that the reign began in 1613 and ended in 1645. So, for the first one, you might picture a *mike* (microphone) in a *hall* and you *shoot* him (613) and make him *roll* (45). See this ridiculous picture and you'll remember that Michael of Russia ruled from 1613 to 1645.

Either *eggs* or *legs* might be your Substitute Word for Alexis. Associate either one with, say, *shrill cash* (645–76).

A *great* letter *P tear*ing a *tie* (the first) would tell you the name: Peter I or Peter the Great. See that tie shaving a pie with a nail; *sh*ave *p*ie nail—689–25.

A *great cat run*ning (Catherine) through *Noah's* (the second) beard, gives you the name. The cat runs into the *kitchen* (762) and hides behind a *bush* (96). If you didn't need a reminder for "the Great" or for "the second," a cat running into the kitchen behind a bush would suffice.

You *pull* (Paul) your *tie* (the first) and a *cabbage* (796) falls out of it onto your *suit* (01).

A *sander* (Alexander) is sanding a ha*t* (the first). You can use *tie* here, but when I have to use a word to represent the same thing many times, I occasionally use a different word, that fits phonetically. The hat is being sanded very *fast* (801) and for the *final* (825) time.

A gigantic *nickel* (Nicholas) is wearing a ha*t* (the first) made of *vinyl* (825) with a large *lily* (55) on it.

A *sander* (Alexander) is sanding *Noah's* beard (the second) until it has a *full* hole (855) of *fat* (81) in it.

Your *Ma* (the third) is a *fat pear* (81–94) and you're *sand*-ing (Alexander) it.

A he*n* (the second) is laying *nickels* (Nicholas) that go up in *vapor* (894) until you *tack* (17) them down.

If you clearly see each of these pictures, you'll know the names and dates. To finish the job, Link the names only in their proper order; that is, mike (Michael) to eggs (Alexis) to *P* tear (Peter), and so on. Once you've done that, you'll know all the names. Then, when you think of a name, the original association you made will tell you the dates of reign.

You can use exactly the same idea to memorize the dynasties of China. Perhaps you wanted to learn this list:

> Prehistoric China
> Chou Dynasty (1027–256 B.C.)
> Ch'in Dynasty (221–207 B.C.)
> Han Dynasty (202 B.C.–A.D. 221)
> T'ang Dynasty (618–906)
> Ming Dynasty (1368–1644)

You can associate the dates with the dynasties first, then Link them, or vice versa; it doesn't matter. I probably would Link them first. I'd start the Link, perhaps, with a picture of Dinah (or a diner) drinking *Chinese* tea; *Dinah's tea*—dynasty.

To start the Link, I might see a *prehistoric* animal coming out of the tea. The prehistoric animal turns out to be a *chow* (or it waits on a chow line) and reminds me of the Chou Dynasty; the chow bites me on the *chin* (Ch'in Dynasty) and then on the *hand* (Han Dynasty). Or you might want to picture a hand growing out of your chin. A gigantic hand is in a *tank* (T'ang Dynasty), or is saying *thanks;* there's a *mink* (Ming Dynasty) in the tank.

Any Link using your own Substitute Words and your own ridiculous pictures will do the job. You will then want to associate the dates with the Substitute Word you're using for each dynasty.

You'd probably know which dates are B.C. and which are A.D., but if you need a reminder for B.C., you might use *back, buck, big,* or *Bic* (pen) to represent it, and put it into your association. *Ad*ding something, or an *ad*vertisement, would remind you of A.D.—although you don't need a reminder for both; one will suffice.

Now see if you can memorize the dates without my help. You're much better off doing it yourself, anyway.

Quite a few students told me that remembering the major wars and the dates would be a great help in the study of history. If you understand the Substitute Word (or thought) idea, and if you know the phonetic sounds, this should be no problem for you. Here are some of the wars and dates listed in a study guide for high school and college history students (it is not a complete list):

> War of Devolution, 1667–1668
> Dutch War, 1672–1678
> Great Northern War, 1700–1721
> War of the Spanish Succession, 1701–1714
> War of the Polish Succession, 1733–1736
> War of the Austrian Succession, 1740–1748
> Seven Years' War, 1756–1763
> French Revolution and Napoleonic Wars, 1792–1815
> Crimean War, 1854–1855
> Austro-Sardinian War, 1859
> Danish War, 1864
> Franco-Prussian War, 1870–1871

If you wanted to remember these wars in order, by number, you'd use your Peg Words. If the sequence is all you need, simply Link them. In each case, put the wars in the order in which you want to memorize them, before you begin. You must decide whether you want to know them by date, by area of the world, or alphabetically. Assuming you want to learn them as listed above, you can associate each war with its date, or dates, and then Link them.

Devil or *evolution* (or both) would remind you of the War of Devolution. Associate devil with *dish chalk* to remind you of 1667, or just to chalk, if all you need is 67; or to *dish chalk chef* (or *shove*) if you want to remember 1667–68.

Dutch War, 1672–1678. See yourself going out "dutch treat" with a *coin* (72); you're having dinner in a *cave* (78; or *concave*); or use *dish coin cave*.

Great Northern War, 1700–1721. See the *great North Star* sewing sand (*sew sand*—00–21). Simply get a *tack* (17) into the picture if you need the century figures.

War of the Spanish Succession, 1701–1714. Perhaps picturing people crossing a *span* (bridge) in *succession* would remind you of the war. See the people crossing and sitting on a tire (*sit tire*—01–14) and you've got the dates. If you have to be reminded that this was the 1700's, see *tack*s crossing the span.

War of the Polish Succession, 1733–1736. Barber *poles* are marching in *succession*. Associate that with *mummy* or *mom* (33) and *match* (36).

War of the Austrian Succession, 1740–1748. *Horse trains* (Austrian) are *succeeding* when they *raise* (40) the *roof* (48).

Seven Years' War, 1756–1763. A *cow* (7) is fighting with some *ears* (years), or with a calendar; the cow is *ticklish* (1756). All you need is the date the war began, obviously.

French Revolution and Napoleonic Wars, 1792–1815. Picture Napoleon (hand in jacket) or a gigantic napoleon pastry fighting with a *dog bone* (1792) and a *dove tail* (1815). If you don't need the centuries, *bundle* (92–15) would do it.

Crimean War, 1854–1855. Associate *crime* with *lure lily* (54–55), or with lure.

Austro–Sardinian War, 1859. Picture a *horse throw*ing (Austro) a *sardine* into a *dove*'s *lap* (1859).

Danish War, 1864. A great *dane* (dog) is sitting in your *chair* (64).

Franco-Prussian War, 1870–1871. A gigantic *frank* (hot dog) is *pressin'* (Prussian) a *casket* (70–71).

If you've made all the associations and reviewed them well, you should be able to answer any examination questions pertaining to these war names and dates. If the question was "When did the Seven Years' War start?" your ridiculous picture of a cow that's ticklish fighting a calendar tells you that the date is 1756.

If you're asked which war began in 1701 and ended in 1714, the digits 0014 will make you think of sit tire; sit tire will remind you of people (or tacks) crossing a span in succession—the War of the Spanish Succession.

If you want to remember the wars in order, Link devil with Dutch treat with span succession with barber poles with horse trains, and so on. You can, if you want to, associate the participants with the war name. For example, the Siege of Vienna (not listed here) was a war fought by Turkey against Austria and Poland. You might want to picture a *weenie* (Vienna) chasing *turkey*s up a *horse tree* (Austria) and a *pole*.

18

LAW; AMENDMENTS TO THE CONSTITUTION; PRECEDENTS

Would it be helpful if you could memorize all the Amendments to the Constitution of the United States? Perhaps you'd want to remember only some of them. Well, all you need for that are the first twenty-five Peg Words and an understanding of the Substitute Word, or "key word" idea. The key word idea simply means to use only one word or phrase from a thought to bring the entire thought to mind.

Here are the first twenty-five Amendments, by number, and the way I memorized them. I used a key word or thought from each one to remind me of its general content. You can put as much information as you like into each association.

1. *Freedom of religion, speech, press, etc.* A gigantic tie (1) is in church, making a speech; the newspapers are covering the story.

2. *Right to bear arms.* Noah (2) is marching into the ark carrying all kinds of weapons.

3. *Freedom from quartering of soldiers.* Your Ma (3) is refusing to allow soldiers to enter her house.

4. *Guarantees against unreasonable search and seizure.* A gigantic loaf of rye (4) bread is forcibly trying to enter your home in order to search it; an American flag arrives and stops it from doing so.

5. *Privilege against self-incrimination.* Many policemen (law, 5) are on the witness stand at the same time (this is to help make the picture ridiculous). They're all shouting, "I refuse to answer on the grounds that it may incriminate

me!" Or, more simply, a group of policemen is refusing to testify at a hearing.

6. *Right to a speedy trial.* A gigantic shoe (6) is being rushed in and out of courtrooms.

7. *Right to trial by jury.* I simply pictured twelve cows (7) serving on a jury.

8. *Prohibits excessive bail and cruel and unusual punishment.* Somebody is posting bail with a small amount of ivy (8), rather than with all he has.

9. *Peoples' rights retained.* Gigantic bees (9) are stinging people, pulling off their right arms and keeping (retaining) them. (I know it's an awful picture; that's the point, you'll never forget it!)

10. *Residual powers revert to the states.* I pictured large biceps (power) residing between my toes (10), then leaving and going back to state capitol buildings.

11. *Exemption of states from suit.* A tot (11) is trying to sue states (capitol buildings), but the states are indifferent— they're *exempt.*

12. *Method of electing President and Vice President.* Millions of pieces of tin (12) are going to the polls during a presidential election; they all use different methods to vote.

13. *Slavery abolished.* A gigantic tombstone (13) is whipping its slaves, then releasing them.

14. *Protection of citizens' rights.* Everyone has a tire (14) around his right arm for protection.

15. *Right to vote.* A gigantic towel (15) is fighting to enter a voting booth; it insists it has the right to do so.

16. *Income tax.* You're paying your taxes with dishes (16) instead of money. (Now, *that's* ridiculous!)

17. *Election of senators.* Gigantic tacks (17) instead of people, are seated in the Senate, or all the senators sit down and jump up because there's a tack on each seat.

18. *Prohibition.* A gigantic dove (18) is asking for a drink

of whiskey, but he can't get it. Or a bottle of whiskey is flying around like a dove.

19. *Women's suffrage.* Millions of women are bathing in a tub (19); the tub is in a voting booth.

20. *Abolishes the "lame-duck" Congress.* A lame duck is walking up and down a gigantic nose (20), or many lame ducks, with gigantic noses, are ordered out of the Congress, or a gigantic nose orders them out.

21. *Repeal of prohibition.* A gigantic net (21) is full of bottles of whiskey; people are helping themselves to the whiskey and getting drunk.

22. *Limits President's terms in office.* A nun (22) is the President of the United States, but she can't run for office again.

23. *Residents of District of Columbia given vote in presidential elections.* Many (Christopher) Columbuses are writing their names (23) on a ballot, or a column of buses (column bus) is doing the same thing. You might prefer to use *district.* Or perhaps *DC* current is forming your name or initials. The assumption must be that you are familiar with the material if you are studying a subject, so all you need is a simple reminder. If you thought of "Columbia, the Gem of the Ocean" when you read this Amendment, then *gem* could remind you of Columbia. Picturing a gigantic business card (name) being *strict* could remind you of District. Either one would be enough to remind you of the Amendment's number and its content.

24. *Poll tax abolished.* A man playing a fiddle (Nero, 24) is stopped from collecting money from voters at the polls.

25. *Presidential disability and succession.* A gigantic nail (25) takes over as President when the President is disabled, or a gigantic nail disables the President of the United States and then takes over.

Remember that these pictures are the ones I personally would use to remind me of the content of each Amendment.

You're always better off thinking up your own pictures and associations. In that way, you're forcing Original Awareness, and the pictures you make up are more likely to come back to you when you need them.

Form the associations for the Amendments, go over them once or twice, and you'll have them memorized and learned. You should now have no trouble answering a typical law exam question like, "Give the rights provided for in the First, Fourth, and Sixth Amendments, specifying the Amendment in which each right is contained."

First, Fourth, and Sixth would make you think of tie, rye, and shoe. Each of these Peg Words will immediately remind you of the content of the Amendment in question. Tie would make you think of a tie in church (freedom of religion) making a speech (freedom of speech), and newspapers covering the story (freedom of press).

If you don't think that the key thoughts I've suggested give you enough information, include whatever you like in each picture. For instance, in the First Amendment, you might want to include something to remind you of the right to peaceful assembly and the right to petition the government.

In the study (and practice) of law it will be necessary for you to remember important precedents. Applying some of the ideas you've learned in this book should make that easy for you.

In 1964 the case of *Miranda v. United States* established that anyone arrested must be informed of his rights, and that any information secured from a prisoner without his being told his rights is inadmissible as evidence.

Again, assuming that you're familiar with the subject matter, all you will need are some reminders of the date, the names in the case, the judge's name if you wish, and so on.

A *veranda* would remind you of Miranda, or you could picture a *mir*ror on a ve*randa*. The American flag would remind you of the United States. You can picture the flag arguing a case on a veranda in front of a gigantic chair (to remind you of the date—64). You can picture a prisoner (a man in a striped prison suit) being released because the flag refuses to tell him his rights.

The case of *Palsgraf v. Long Island Railroad Co.* established a precedent for future accident cases—that a causal relationship must be shown between an owner's negligence and the accident.

Picture your *pal* putting all his graphs (Palsgraf) onto a *long* train (you can see an *eye land* on the long train, if you like). Your pal has an accident, but the train pulls out of the station anyway, because its negligence had nothing to do with the accident.

Some of my students have memorized books full of precedents this way. Once you've formed your own associations, just hearing about or reading the precedent will remind you of the names and facts involved.

I've used these two precedents as examples because a law student showed me two questions that appeared on one of his exams. One question was: "In 1962 a man was tried for a crime in which his confession to police without his being informed of his right to remain silent was introduced as evidence. Was the confession admissible evidence?"

If you had memorized the *Miranda v. United States* precedent, you would know that that particular precedent was established in 1964. Therefore, the answer to the question is "Yes." In 1962 evidence obtained in this manner was still admissible.

The other question was: "In the case of an accident, is the owner of the premises in which the accident occurred always held responsible?"

Had you memorized the *Palsgraf v. Long Island Railroad* precedent, you'd know that the answer is "No." A causal relationship must be shown between the owner's negligence and the accident before he can be held responsible.

19

HISTORY

A sample question on a college history exam: Identify Uriah Stephens, Haymarket Square, the National Labor Union, Samuel Gompers, the Homestead Steel Plant, Eugene V. Debs, and the Pullman Strike.

Uriah Stephens was the founder of the Knights of Labor in 1869. If you want to remember this fact, associate a Substitute Word or thought for the man's name with a Substitute thought for Knights of Labor. You might picture some *hens* on a *steep* hill (*steep hens*—Stephens), and you're saying, *"You're higher"* (Uriah). This scene takes place at *night* and the hens are busy at their *labor* (Knights of Labor). If you see them laboring on a *ship* (69) you will also know the date.

Chicago's *Haymarket Square* was the scene of a rally by members of the Knights of Labor when they protested the death of a striker at a previous fracas. A bomb exploded here, killing seven people. Picture a *hay market* in a *square* (or boxing ring) with lots of *knights* (in armor) *labor*ing as they protest; you can see one of them lying dead to remind you of the death of a striker. See a bomb exploding among the knights and a *cow* (7) dying.

The *National Labor Union* was created in 1866 by William Sylvis. This was the first federation of unions in contrast to the usual separate unions for separate crafts. It later became the National Labor Reform Party, which disappeared after the 1872 election. Picture all the *labor*ers in the country (national) joining hands on a train (*choo choo*—66); the train is riding on a gigantic *bill* (William), which turns *silver*

121

(Sylvis). There's a party in progress on this silver bill; all the laborers of the country jump down and re-form (reshape) it. The entire party disappears as a gigantic *coin* (72) falls on it.

Samuel Gompers was the founder (1886) of the American Federation of Labor. He was its president almost continuously until his death in 1924. The A. F. of L. took the place of the Knights of Labor. Picture a *mule* (Samuel) in *rompers* (Gompers) finding a large *fish* (86). The fish waves an American flag as it feeds rations (*fed a ration*) to *labor*ers (American Federation of Labor). You can use anything you like, of course; an *ape* (*A*) breaking off *half* (*F*) of an *el* (*L*) train is just as good. The fish becomes president of the laborers and plays a fiddle (*Nero*—24). All people in armor (knights) are replaced by fish (or American flags).

The *Homestead Steel Plant* was the scene of an attack by strikers on 3,000 private guards who were there to protect strikebreakers. You might picture someone *steal*ing a *home* in*stead* of a *plant* and being struck by a lone (private) mouse; the *mouse sues* (3000).

Eugene V. Debs was the head of the American Railway Union. He became nationally known during the Pullman Strike, and ran for President five times on the Socialist Party ticket. You can picture *debs* (debutantes) to remind you of the name; debs eating veal (*V*) in their *jeans* (Eugene) would remind you of the entire name. You might see American flags coming out of the debs' heads and getting on trains (railway) in order to join each other (head of American Railway Union). They do join together and *pull* a *man* in and strike him as the whole country watches (became nationally known during the Pullman Strike). The man tries to run away five times (or runs to the *law*), but he's caught and forced to *socialize* at a *party*.

The *Pullman Strike* was the strike by workers at Pullman's palace car factory; the strikers were later joined by the members of the American Railway Union. The strike is significant because President Cleveland, on pretext of ensuring the movement of mail, sent troops to preserve order. You might picture men refusing to work as they're pulled (*pull man*) to their jobs; picture American flags coming by rail to help pull the workers the other way. So many troops arrive that they *cleave* the *land* (Cleveland); this keeps things in order as tons of mail fall out of the "cleaved" land.

20

HOW TO MEMORIZE A MAP (THE "MEMORY GRAPH")

Throughout school it would help if you could memorize the locations of places on maps. There are, as usual, a variety of ways to do it. Before I go into what I consider the best way, the "memory graph," I'll discuss the obvious way. I can't think of a better example than the map of the United States, since you'd have to know the approximate locations of fifty different places (the states) in order to have the map memorized.

This is another use of the Link system of memory in conjunction with the Substitute Word idea. You can memorize the map by forming six Links, which will give you the approximate location of each state. Here they are:

You can see that I have simply listed the states in their approximate locations, in columns. Just doing that will give you a general picture of where the states are located. True memory will tell you exactly where they belong—*if* you have a reminder. And the Links are your reminder!

You may want to list them just a bit differently. Some are in columns together that are not one under the other on the map, but right next to each other. Illinois and Indiana, for example. As I said, true memory will tell you the difference.

You can list the states in fewer or more Links. You might decide to set them in eight columns instead of six, like this:

ALASKA		MONTANA	NORTH DAKOTA	MINNESOTA			MAINE
WASHINGTON	IDAHO	WYOMING	SOUTH DAKOTA	IOWA	WISCONSIN	MICHIGAN	VERMONT
OREGON	NEVADA	COLORADO	NEBRASKA	MISSOURI	ILLINOIS	INDIANA	NEW HAMPSHIRE
CALIFORNIA	UTAH	NEW MEXICO	KANSAS	ARKANSAS	TENNESSEE	OHIO	NEW YORK
HAWAII	ARIZONA		OKLAHOMA	LOUISIANA	MISSISSIPPI	KENTUCKY	MASSACHUSETTS
			TEXAS			ALABAMA	CONNECTICUT
							NEW JERSEY
							RHODE ISLAND
							PENNSYLVANIA
							DELAWARE
							MARYLAND
							WEST VIRGINIA
							VIRGINIA
							NORTH CAROLINA
							SOUTH CAROLINA
							GEORGIA
							FLORIDA

You might also want to break down that last column into two columns.

I don't want to go through all the Links and all the Substitute Words; I think you can do that on your own. Just think up a Substitute Word (or thought) for each state, then Link them. That's all there is to it.

If you want to, you can form one continuous Link of the states, putting something into your picture that will tell you where a Link ends—for example, a stop sign. Once you've formed your Link or Links and reviewed them a few times, you'll be able to draw a map showing all the states of the Union in their proper places!

Here's another method that I think is even better. The same method can be used for other studies—for instance, whenever you have to remember the locations of things on graphs or tables.

	1.		2.		3.	
A	ALASKA WASHINGTON OREGON	MONTANA IDAHO WYOMING	NORTH DAKOTA SOUTH DAKOTA MINNESOTA	WISCONSIN MICHIGAN INDIANA	MAINE NEW HAMPSHIRE VERMONT NEW YORK NEW JERSEY	MASSACHUSETTS CONNECTICUT RHODE ISLAND PENNSYLVANIA
B	CALIFORNIA NEVADA	UTAH COLORADO	NEBRASKA KANSAS IOWA	MISSOURI ILLINOIS	MARYLAND DELAWARE OHIO WEST VIRGINIA	VIRGINIA KENTUCKY TENNESSEE NORTH CAROLINA
C	CALIFORNIA ARIZONA	NEW MEXICO HAWAII	TEXAS OKLAHOMA	ARKANSAS LOUISIANA	SOUTH CAROLINA MISSISSIPPI FLORIDA	ALABAMA GEORGIA

In this table the country is broken into nine sections. Northwest (A1); West (B1); Southwest (C1) North Central states (A2); Central states (B2); South Central states (C2); Northeast (A3); East (B3); Southeast (C3).

Now here's the very simple idea. All you need is a word to represent each section. The words will be easy to remember because each one will begin with the letter, and will have as its next consonant sound the sound that represents the number.

The word for A1 is *ate*. Do you see why? *Ate* begins with *A* and the next consonant sound is *T*, which, as you know, can represent only number 1. So *ate* can represent only A1.

The word for A2 must also begin with *A*, but the consonant sound must be *N*, for 2. The word I use is *awn* (to cover with an awning). The word for A3 is *aim*; it begins with *A*, and the consonant sound for number 3 is *M*.

B1—bat	C1—cat
B2—bean	C2—can
B3—bomb	C3—comb

Go over all of them once or twice, and you'll know them. Now, how do you use them? This way: Link all the states in section A1 to *ate*—that's all. There are two ways to do it. Start your Link with *ate* (eating), and continue with your Substitute Words for the states. Do the same with all the sections.

Another way is to associate *ate* (or eating) with each of the states in section A1, and *awn* with each of the states in section A2, and so on. Either method will work. Once you've made your Links or associations, you'll know all the states, and where they are located.

When you want to know, say, the South Central states, picture the graph in your mind. Since the South Central states are in section C2, C2 will automatically make you think of *can,* and *can* will tell you the states in that area.

If you have to know where, say, Indiana is located, you may have a silly picture in your mind of an *Indian* wearing an *awn*ing. That tells you that Indiana is in section A2, because *awn* can represent only A2, the North Central area. A picture of you *carry*ing a *line* (Carolina) of *bomb*s (B3) in a storm (north) tells you that North Carolina is part of the Eastern section of the country.

You will notice, by the way, that California is listed in both B1 and C1. That is to remind you that California is a long state and is part of both the West and the Southwest.

Of course, you can list the states in any way you wish and Link them in any order you wish. You can enlarge the graph with a fourth line and column if you like, and that will pinpoint the location of the states even more. For some areas or countries of the world, you might need only four sections: A1, A2, B1, and B2. It's up to you.

Once you understand the idea of the memory graph, you can superimpose the map of any country onto it and form your associations. You'll see that it works well, and you'll find many other uses for it, too.

If you want to remember the capitals of the states, you can simply associate your Substitute Word for the state with a Substitute Word for the capital city. Example: you're *mix*ing something *again* (Michigan) and something *lands sing*ing (Lansing) into the mixture.

The system can be applied to any country. A picture of *many germs boiling* tells you that the capital of East Germany is East Berlin. If you need a reminder for East, put *yeast* in your picture.

Would it help to know, say, the important rivers of a country? Simply form Substitute Words for their names and Link them in the order that would remind you of their location. You can also include the names of the cities they flow through in your picture. Merely start a Link with the name of the river and Link the cities to that.

A Link of *pass a fig, add land tick, Indian,* and *arc* would tell you the names of the four great oceans: Pacific, Atlantic, Indian, and Arctic.

A Link of the seven continents in size order could be: *a chair* (Asia), *a free car* (Africa), *a merry car* in a *storm*

(North America), another *merry car* with a big *mouth* (South America), an *ant* doing *art*work in *a car* (Antarctica), *you rope* (Europe), and *ass* (*donkey*) *trail ya'*, or a kangaroo (Australia).

To learn the exports of a country, form an association between the name of the country and the product. A *whale* squirting a geyser of oil from its blowhole would remind you that Venezuela (whale) exports oil, for example.

21

MATHEMATICS AND MEASURES

In the previously published *Good Memory—Good Student!*, in which I used elementary-school study examples, I showed younger students how to memorize the multiplication table. All that's necessary is to make up a word for a problem and associate that word with another that represents the answer. For instance, associating *cap* with *jam* would tell the student that $7 \times 9 = 63$ and associating *ship* with *lure* that $6 \times 9 = 54$. The multiplication table is, in the beginning, a memory problem. If you still have a bit of trouble with it, you might try applying the system.

Understanding and knowing the sounds of the phonetic alphabet makes it easy to remember numbers of any kind. It probably isn't necessary for you to memorize cube roots and cubes, but now you can do it in a very short time, if you want to. Many of my students memorized all the cubes from 1 to 100 in less than an hour.

A few examples: The cube of 18 is 5,832. A silly picture of a dove (18) in *love* with the *moon* would etch this into your memory. I'd suggest you use one word (your basic Peg Word, if you like) for the cube root and then any word or phrase, that fits phonetically, for the cube. Form a good strong association between the two, and you've got it.

The cube of 21 is 9,261. Associate *net, knot,* or *nut* with *punched, pinched,* or *punished.*

28; 21,952. A waiter is handing you a plane instead of a knife and you say, "K*nife, not plane.*"

34; 39,304. Associate *mower* with *mop miser.*

35; 42,875. *Mu*le with *rain vocal* or *ran off coal.*

37; 50,653. A gigantic *mug* catches lots of lice and jails 'em; *lice jail 'em.*

41; 68,921. Associate *rod* with *shove paint* or *shave point*.

44; 85,184. *Rower* with *fool diver* or *fill too far*.

45; 91,125. *Roll* with *pit tunnel* or *bite toenail*.

51; 132,651. *Lot* with *domain jeweled*.

52; 140,608. See a *lion* tearing its shoes off; *tears shoes off*.

56; 175,616. Associate *lash* or *leech* with *tackle jet age*.

64; 262,144. Associate *chair* with *no chain* (or *inchin'*) *terror* (or *dreary*).

68; 314,432. *Chef* with *motor roomin'* (or *meter remain*).

75; 421,875. Associate *kill* with *runt fickle* (or *vocal*).

83; 571,787. *Foam* with *licked* (or *liked*) *cave cow* (or *key fake*). '

85; 614,125. *Foil* with *ashtray tunnel* (or *toenail*).

91; 753,571. *Bat* with *climb locate* (or *clam liked*).

94; 830,584. Picture a *bear* being a *famous lover*.

95; 857,375. Associate *bell* with *flick mogul* (or *Michael*).

If you've seen these pictures clearly, then you know the cubes of all these numbers. Just as an exercise, it wouldn't be a bad idea for you to try to memorize all the cubes from 1 to 100.

This may seem too elementary to you, yet I'm aware of the fact that many students do not know the decimal equivalents of fractions, except the obvious ones like ¼, ½, and ¾. Of course, you can work out the decimal equivalents if you have to, but it would certainly save you lots of time if you had the table of fractions and their decimal equivalents right at the tip of your mind.

Use the same idea as for the cubes and cube roots. All you have to do is to use any word (the Peg Word will do) that fits phonetically to represent the fraction and then associate that with any word or phrase that will remind you of the decimal (or percent) equivalent.

Here are some examples:

⅕ = .20 (20%). Form one fast, simple, ridiculous association between, say, towel and nose, and you won't forget it. A towel hanging from your nose will do. Towel can only represent 15, or ⅕ in this case, and nose can only represent 20 or .20.

⅙ = .16⅔. Since the decimal equivalents of the sixths end in thirds, it isn't necessary to include the 3 in the association. What you need to be reminded of is how *many* thirds there are. Associate *dish* (⅙) with either *dashin'* or (*touch knee*). You can either use a word or phrase that includes the entire number you want to remember—162 (.16⅔)—or you can use one word for the main number (16) and another to tell you how many thirds (2). Either way will work.

⅐ = .14 2/7. The decimal equivalents of sevenths end in sevenths, so all you need is a reminder of how many sevenths there are. Seeing a *tack* in your *terrain* (or *train*) would do it; or a *tack* is a *tree now*.

⅛ = .125 (12½%). All the decimal equivalents of eighths end in ½, or the digit 5, so you can omit that from your association if you like, or leave it in, it doesn't matter. Picturing a *dove* (⅛) in a *tunnel* (125) would do it.

⅑ = .11⅑. Picture an old *tub;* it's *dated* (111—11 and 1 ninth).

I'm sure you see how simple it all is by now. After you've formed your associations for the fractions and decimal equivalents that you want to remember, all you have to do is go over them once or twice and you'll know them all. After a few uses, the ridiculous pictures will fade—they will have served their purpose. The information will have become knowledge.

Measures

Applying the systems to metric measures takes no time at all. If it is important for you to know that a millimeter is .03937 inches, form an association between a girl named *Milly,* or a *mill* of *meters,* and *sum* up *mug,*" and you've got it. If you feel it's necessary to be reminded of inches, get *itch* or *inch*worm into the picture. So, your picture might be of a mill where meters are coming off the assembly line, and a mug counts them—he's the "sum up mug"—and he's scratching himself because he has an itch. This takes time to write, but it's really an instantaneous picture. See it clearly, and you'll always know that a millimeter is .03937 inches.

Picture a gigantic *key* bent *low* (kilometer) being a *janitor* with a s*mile,* and you'll know that a kilometer is .6214 miles.

Picture yourself *pound*ing (or *dog pound*) a *real match* (4536) while the *gram*ophone is playing, and that will help you recall that a pound is 453.6 grams.

A *mule* (*mile* or *smile*) *touches* up (1609) a *key* that's *low.* That association will help you remember that a mile is 1.609 kilometers.

I've disregarded the decimal points in these examples because you should know where they go. The assumption is that if the facts are important to you, you will already know the approximate figures. The system makes it more definite. You can, if you like, make up a picture to represent the decimal point—say, the point of a knife—and put that into the association at the proper place. For instance, in the last example, you can picture a mule (mile) wearing a tie (1); it sticks a knife point (decimal point) into the tie to *jazz* (it) u*p* (609).

Another measure you might want to remember is the earth's diameter, which is 7,927 miles. Picture a *gaping* hole in the earth and a dime (diameter) falling into it.

The speed of sound is 742 miles per hour. See a *crown* traveling through the air, making lots of noise (sounds).

The speed of light is 186,282 miles per second. See a whi*te-fish* having *no fun* in a *light* bulb.

22

FORMULAS

All formulas and equations are sequences; therefore, you'd use the Link system to memorize them. With the aid of the phonetic alphabet, the alphabet Peg Words, and the Substitute Word idea, you can form a Link for any formula.

The formula for finding the area of a regular polygon is:

$$\frac{1}{4} \ NL^2 \ cot \ \frac{180}{N}$$

Of course, you can probably find the area of a regular polygon without knowing the formula. You can work out the formula, if you understand the concept of polygons to begin with. I'm using it only as an example. A simple Link will etch the formula into your mind and memory easily and quickly.

In every case, the Link for a formula should start with (or include) a Substitute Word for what the formula represents. It would be silly to memorize a formula without knowing its application.

For this example, you can picture a *polly* (parrot) that's *gone* (lost) in a large *area*. This tells you that the rest of the Link refers to the formula for finding the area of a polygon. The rest of the Link might be: There's a *quarte*r (¼) where the polly was; the quarter is *kneelin'* (NL^2) on a *cot* near a *hen* (N; alphabet Peg Word); the hen is being attacked from above (over) by *doves* (180).

I pictured a twenty-five-cent piece to represent one quarter; I usually do. NL^2 made me think of *kneelin'*, so kneelin' will remind me of NL^2. You might have seen the quarter kneeling on a *square* cot. All right. Cot, of course, will remind you of cot in the formula. The hen will remind you of *N*, and doves attacking from above will remind you that 180 goes *over* the *N*. On the other hand, you could make up a standard for "divided by" instead of "over."

When you start applying the system to formulas, you'll need some standards for certain symbols. They'll fall into place automatically once you start applying the system. I always use an American flag to represent the equal sign, because in America, all people are supposed to be equal.

I use a *mynah* bird or a *miner* to represent the minus sign, *applause* (or *applesauce*) to represent the plus sign (because it sounds a bit like it), and a *tree* to remind me of square root.

The formula for harmonic motion is:

$$T = 2\pi\,\sqrt{\dfrac{M}{K}}$$

To remember it, I formed this quick Link: A *harmonica* that's *moving* (harmonic motion) is drinking *tea* (*T*); the cup of tea is waving an American flag. (Most often, you'll know where the equal sign belongs, and won't need a reminder.) Each of *two pies* (2π) is waving a flag; pies are growing on a tree (square root), and the tree is driving a Mack truck.

The *M*ack truck reminds me of *M* over *K*. You can see the truck going *over* the tree, if you like, or you can associate tree with ham (*M*) on a cake (*K*). If you've made this Link, harmonic motion should make you think of tea (*T*). Tea should make you think of American flag (=), and flag should make you think of two pies (2π). Pies should make you think of tree (square root), and tree should make you think of Mack (*M* over *K*).

The point is that you now have something tangible to picture in your mind. It is difficult (if at all possible) to picture the formula itself at first. The system gives you a way to picture it. It makes the intangible tangible, or meaningful. Equally important, it forces you to concentrate on the formula.

If a formula consists of letters only, it's that much easier to Link. For a formula like this: $P(K\ def) = (\frac{N}{K})\ (P)^k\ (P)^{n-k}$ you could picture yourself poking a deaf man (*poke deaf— PK* def) with an American flag (=); the flag has a vertical *nick* $(\frac{N}{K})$ in it, out of which *peeks* (P^k) a *pink* (P^{n-k}) eye.

If you want to include a reminder of the parentheses you can use *bowlegs* as your standard. You can also see the eye peeking *up* to remind you that the components (k and n–k) belong near the top of the P's.

Quadratic formula: $\quad X = \dfrac{-b \pm \sqrt{b^2 - 4^{ac}}}{2a}$

Start the Link with something to remind you of quadratic; perhaps *aquatic,* or *quad*ruplets in an *attic.* Associate that with some *eggs* (X) waving a flag (=). A *miner* (–) is waving a flag; *b*eans (*b*) fly out of the miner's head and another miner applauds over (±) his head; the applauding miner climbs a tree (square root) and goes into a *bin* (b^2); a *my*nah bird (–) flies out of the bin pushing a clothes *rack* (4ac; true memory should tell you that *rack* represents 4ac and not Rac) over (to remind you of the dividing line) Noah (2) who is wrestling an *ape* (*a*).

For 2a, you could also picture yourself saying "*Na,* you'll never make it," to the mynah bird. See the pictures you decide on and you'll have learned the formula.

The formula for total energy is: $\quad E = \dfrac{-M\ (\pi K\ Q_1\ Q_2)^2}{N^2\ h^2}$ —

You might Link an *energetic ee*l to flag (and to *ladder* to remind you of over, or put it into the link at the end of the part of the formula that's above the line) to *miner* to *ham* to *pike*

(πk) to *quit* (Q_1) to *queen* (Q_2) to *n*ew or *n*o, or to a *boxing ring* to remind you of *squared,* (over) to *n*oon (N^2) to *h*en (h^2). I've given you the words; remember, you must form the pictures. Even if you don't have to know this formula, try it and see how easy it is.

The formula for electric charge (Q) is:

$$Q = 6.25 \times 10^{-18} \text{ charges} = 1 \text{ coulomb}$$

These words would remind you of the components: cue, flag, channel *New York Times* (if you think you need a reminder for X), tossed off or test of (get miner in there if you want to be reminded of the minus sign), charges, tie (1), column.

The pictures to match might be: a *cue* stick is waving a *flag;* a gigantic flag is crossing the (English) *channel;* a large (Sunday) *Times* is crossing the channel as a *test of* strength; *charges* of electricity fly out of its muscles (strength); the electricity destroys many *flags;* millions of *ties* fall out of the flags; the ties form one gigantic *column.*

When there are words rather than symbols in any formula, simply use Substitute Words for them. One of the formulas for a form of alcohol is:

1,1 diphenyl 2,2 dimethyl 1,2 ethanediol

To memorize it form this Link: as a *tot* (1,1) died he fanned a large letter *L* (*die fan L*—diphenyl; or *dippin' L*); a *nun* (2,2) also fanned the *L;* the nun gave a dime to Ethel (*dime Ethel*—dimethyl; or *dime is ill*); Ethel couldn't lift the dime because it weighed a *ton* (1,2), so she "et" (ate) it as she aimed at an old man; he died (*et aim die old*—ethanediol; or *attain dial*). See these pictures, and you'll have memorized this formula in hardly any time at all.

It doesn't matter what components appear in a formula; you

can *always* make up a picture that would remind you of it. For delta ($\triangle$), *dealt a* (dealing cards); for curvilinear ($\S$), a pitcher throwing a *curve* would do; for vector ($\rightleftharpoons$), *victor* or *victory,* or half an arrow; and so on. Once you understand that, you can Link (picture) any component in any formula.

In electrical physics, this formula is used in solving electric intensity fields:

$$\oint \vec{E} \cdot d\vec{S} = 4\pi \ KQ$$

The first thoughts that come to my mind are these: a pitcher is throwing a *curve* to an *eel;* the eel hits the ball and holds up its hand in the *victory* sign; a *period* runs out on the field and *dies* as it, too, gives the *victory* sign; a *flag* is waved over the period; a *raw pie* (4π) falls out of the flag; you hit the pie with a *cane* (K) and a *cue* (Q) stick (or until the pie yells, "Quit").

One high school student told me that the formulas to find the trigonometric ratios of an angle must be memorized. Although they're quite simple, his teacher felt it necessary to give the students a mnemonic aid. The formulas are:

$$\sin = \frac{\text{opposite}}{\text{hypotenuse}} \qquad \cos = \frac{\text{adjacent}}{\text{hypotenuse}} \qquad \tan = \frac{\text{opposite}}{\text{adjacent}}$$

The mnemonic is *sohcahtoa.* The problem, as usual, is to remember this nonsense word itself, and what it represents. *Soak a toe, soak ah toe,* or *sew car to A* all make sense, can be pictured, and will remind you of the nonsense word. Associate any of them with a Substitute Word or phrase that will remind you of trigonometric ratios of an angle.

You can also form a definite link to remind you of the letters. Perhaps a *trigger* is driving a *radio* around an *ess* curve (S) that has lots of *angles*; the curve is so sharp, it makes you say "Oh!" (OH). As you say it, you finish the curve and see the *sea* (*C*) and you say "Ah!" (*AH*). As you say that you drive straight *to*ward an *ape,* or an *A* (*TOA*).

I've mentioned this only to show you some methods of handling these things. The easiest way for this particular problem is to associate sign with opposite with pot (a gigantic *sign* is *opposite* a gigantic *pot*—sin = opposite over hypotenuse). A *coat signs* (cosine) as it stands *adjacent* to a *pot;* a *tan gent* is tanning his *opposite* side with a lamp that *a J sent.*

There are more examples of how to remember different kinds of formulas and equations in other chapters.

Incidentally, I assume you know by now how to remember simple pieces of information like pi = 3.1416. Picture a *pie* in a *mightier dish,* and you've got it. *Mad radish* or *motor touch* would do just as well.

23

MORE MATHEMATICS

In a high school algebra textbook, the student is often told to memorize type forms like these:

1. $a(X + Y) = aX + aY$
2. $(X + Y)(X - Y) = X^2 - Y^2$
3. $(X + Y)^2 = X^2 + 2 \times Y + Y^2$
4. $(X - Y)^2 = X^2 - 2 \times Y + Y^2$
5. $(X + a)(X + b) = X^2 + (a + b)X + ab$

Use your Peg Words to learn them by number:

1. A tie (1) swings an axe and a bottle of wine applauds $[a(X + Y)]$; an American flag (=) also applauds as another axe applauds and says, "Ay" $[= aX + aY]$. There are always other ways to handle a problem. In this case, you might want to use *taxi axe A* to remind you of the equation, the *T* for number 1, and the other letters for the equation itself.

2. Noah (2) eats many eggs $[(X)$ plus wine $[+ Y)]$; one of the eggs digs (mines) for more wine $[(X - Y)]$; an American flag mines with oxen $[X^2]$ as another miner emits a yawn $[-Y^2]$.

3. Some eggs applaud $[(X +]$ your Ma's (3) big yawn $[Y)^2]$; so does an American flag (=); some oxen $[X^2]$ wave a flag and applaud a hen $[+ 2]$ who is reading the *Times* and drinking wine $[XY]$; the wine applauds as the hen yawns $[+ Y^2]$.

4. This one is easy. Associate rye (4) to Ma (3) and simply set your mind to the fact that this type form is the same as number 3 except that the first two plus signs change to minus signs.

5. Some eggs who are policemen (law; 5) applaud an ape;

some other eggs applaud a bean $[(X+a)(X+b)]$; the bean waves an American flag (=) as oxen applaud $[X^2+]$; an ape applauds a bean $[(a+b)]$; the bean reads the *Times,* which applauds Abe $[X+ab]$.

These Links will remind you of the type forms. Of course, if you prefer, you can memorize the wording rather than the equations. For example, type form number 2 above would read: The product of the sum of two numbers by their difference is equal to the difference of their squares.

You'd be reminded of it by forming this Link: Two gigantic numbers are reading the *Times* and being applauded by miners (the sum of two numbers times their difference); the miners wave American flags (=) in different boxing rings (difference of their squares; I use boxing ring as a standard picture for square).

I wanted to give you just an idea of how to handle the equations in both forms. Again, the assumption is that you're familiar with what you're trying to memorize, and all you really need are *reminders.*

Any law or theorem can be memorized using the Link and Substitute Word ideas. In trigonometry, you may want to remember the law of sines and the law of cosines.

The law of sines: In a triangle the ratio of any side to the sine of the opposite angle is constant. To be reminded of this, you might start a Link with a picture of large signs being policemen (the law of sines), or of signs being the members of a jury. Assuming you thought of the latter, see that jury of signs sitting in a triangle instead of a jury box. Continuing the Link, picture a radio (ratio) on a side of the triangle; opposite the radio is a sign with a halo (angel, to remind you of angle); that halo never moves; it remains constant.

The law of cosines: In a triangle the square of any side is

equal to the sum of the squares of the other two sides minus twice the product of those sides and the cosine of the angle included between them.

You might start the Link with a picture of a policeman (law) cosigning a contract written on a triangular piece of paper. The triangular paper flies into a boxing ring (square) and fights at any side; it waves an American flag (is equal to) as it fights; some other boxing rings (sum of the squares) come from two sides (of the other two sides); a mynah bird reads two *Times* (minus twice the product) on the sides of these other boxing rings; then it cosigns, with an angel, the contract lying between them (and the cosine of the angle included between them).

Another trigonometric theorem: The sine, cosine, secant, and cosecant functions have the period 2π. The tangent and cotangent functions have the period π.

A large sign (sine) is cosigning (cosine) a contract; it takes a second (secant) and a coat runs over for a second (cosecant), makes a period and gets *two pies* (2π) in the face; a *tan gent* (tangent) wearing a *coat* (cotangent) attends a function where he is served *one pie, period* (period π).

Please pardon the repetition, but I must tell you again that since you'd be studying the subject, you'd already be familiar with the material and the short Links would "lock it in" for you. I also want to remind you that I've suggested the first words and pictures that came to my mind; what you think of would probably be much better for you. Forming the Links helps to etch the information into your mind. It forces Original Awareness.

If you form a few standards for certain words, you can form associations or Links to help you remember and learn any trigonometric or geometric theorem. For example, you might always picture railroad tracks to represent the word "parallel"; a *pair of L's* would also do. A train reversing might represent "transversal"; a pen standing on its end could represent "perpendicular"; the phrase *con grew ant,* or just *grew ant* (and whatever it conjures up in your mind), might be your reminder for "congruent." I usually use a bent piece of metal to represent "angle"; you can use that, or angel. Half a grapefruit could always represent "half," and so on. Once you think of a picture or two for any word, you'll usually think of it when you come across that word again; then it has become a "standard" for you.

If two parallel lines are cut by a transversal, each pair of corresponding angles are congruent.

To learn the preceding, you might form this Link: A train reverses (transversal) and cuts both railroad tracks (two parallel lines); this separates two (a pair) angels who must now correspond about their hobby of growing ants (corresponding angles are congruent).

In a plane, if a line is perpendicular to one of two parallel lines, it is perpendicular to the other.

In an airplane, a clothesline is standing on end parallel to a pen that's standing on end. Picture it being perpendicular to another pen.

Through a given point there passes one and only one line perpendicular to a given plane.

Someone is giving you a sharp point; one clothesline that has a pen standing on end on it passes through this point and gives you an airplane.

Two lines perpendicular to the same plane are coplanar.

Picture two clotheslines (you can use *lions* for lines, if you like) standing on end on the same airplane; the two lines are planning something (coplanar).

If one leg of a right triangle is half as long as the hypotenuse, then the opposite angle has measure 30.

You might see a triangle (the musical instrument) throwing a punch (right cross); the triangle has two legs, one of which is half as long as the other (you can see the other leg being a pot, to remind you of hypotenuse). With this, associate an angel sitting (opposite angle) on a *m*ouse (30) and measuring it with a ruler.

If two triangles have the same altitude *h*, then the ratio of their areas is equal to the ratio of their bases.

Two triangles are floating at the same altitude; each has an ache (*h*; or an itch); a radio (ratio) is running all over the area (of the triangles) waving an American flag (equal) as another radio runs around the bases.

A plane perpendicular to a radius at its outer end is tangent to the sphere.

A pen on its end is flying around like an airplane, carrying radios (radius) at its outer end; a tan man (tangent) comes out of a radio carrying a large sphere.

The segment between the midpoints of two sides of a triangle is parallel to the third side and half as long.

Picture railroad tracks (parallel) coming toward each other from the centers (midpoint) of two sides of a triangle; they go over your Ma (third side) and make her half as long as she used to be (or they go over your Ma who is eating half a grapefruit).

A Pythagorean theorem (for right triangles only) in equation form is:

$$C^2 = a^2 + b^2$$

This is a simple equation and it can be memorized with a simple Link. You might start the Link by picturing yourself throwing a right cross at a triangle (right triangle). Out of the triangle comes a can (C^2) waving an American flag (=) as Ann applauds (a^2 +) a gigantic bean (b^2).

To memorize the equation for the law of cosines, all you have to do is lengthen the Link you just formed (or form a separate one). The equation is:

$$C^2 = a^2 + b^2 - 2ab \cos < C$$

Start your Link with a Substitute Word for cosine; perhaps a *can* is cosigning a contract. Continue the Link as above up to "bean"; now the bean tries to nab a miner ($-2ab$) who goes (cos) at an angle ($<$) into the sea (C).

Ordinarily it would appear to be an impossible task to memorize the table of trigonometric ratios. Applying the phonetic alphabet and the idea of association, however, transforms it into a fairly easy chore. Whether or not it would help you in your studies to memorize the table is something you must decide.

I don't think it's necessary to reproduce the entire table here. Since you already know how to handle numbers, one or two examples should suffice. Part of the table would look like this:

r	sin r	cos r	tan r
20°	.342	.940	.364
32°	.530	.848	.625
57°	.839	.545	1.540

Forming a Link starting with the degree, and working in sin, cos, tan order in each case, solves the problem. You needn't put anything into the Links to remind you of sin, cos, or tan because the words or phrases will be in that order each time and you'll know, automatically, which is which.

You might make your first link *nose* to *marine* (or *maroon*) to *brass* to *major* or *my chair*. The next link: *moon* to *looms* to *far off* to *channel;* the moon looms far off over the channel—but be sure to make it ridiculous. The last example: *lake* to *foam up* to *laurel* to *tailors, dollars,* or *toilers.*

That's all there is to it. It wouldn't take you too much time or effort to learn the entire table of trigonometric ratios this way, if you wanted to.

24

BIOLOGY AND GENETICS

Part of the difficulty in learning almost any subject is the necessity to remember terminology. Biology is a good example of this problem. In a college textbook on the subject, the author tells the student to put his mind to the terminology first, so that he'll understand what he reads and what his instructor is talking about.

For example, if you're studying cells and cell morphology, you'll probably have to know the terminology for the parts of a typical animal cell section. The names of these parts are: golgi body, centriole, nucleolus, nuclear membrane, cell membrane, mitochondrion, cytoplasm, and chromatin.

It's easy enough to form a Link of Substitute Words that will remind you of these names. Start the Link with any picture that will remind you of *cell,* perhaps a prison cell, with an animal in it.

The animal in the cell has a *gold (gee!) body;* a *cent* that's *roll*ing has, or is picked up by, a gold body; you use a cent to buy a *new Cleo* (goldfish), and you *lose* it. You find a *new clear* fish with a *brain;* the new clear fish is thrown into a *cell* with a *brain;* in that cell is a catcher's *mitt* that's *talkin' and dryin'* (dishes, perhaps). The mitt *sit*s on your *toe*s and gives you *plasm*a; a gigantic toe sits on a sheet of *chrome* that's really *tin.*

If you formed ridiculous pictures in your mind while you were reading, or if you go back now and imagine them, you'll see how simple it all is. You will have learned the parts of a typical animal cell section in hardly any time at all.

During the study of biology or genetics, you learn that genes

147

are made up of DNA and RNA. DNA stands for deoxyribonucleic acid; RNA is ribonucleic acid. If you remember what DNA stands for, you'll also know the meaning of RNA, since it's the same except for "deoxy."

Knowing the alphabet Peg Words makes it easy to form a picture that represents DNA. A dean (*D*) holding a hen (*N*) in one hand and an ape (*A*) in the other would do it. Or you could simply picture a girl named *Dinah*; that should be enough to remind you of DNA.

Dinah is putting a large *D* on an *ox;* she ties it on with a *ribbon* that's *new* and *clear*. That ridiculous picture should suffice to remind you that DNA is deoxyribonucleic acid. As I said, it will also tell you what RNA stands for, but if you want to associate that too, you can picture an a*rena* (RNA) full of *ribbons,* all *new* and *clear*.

This same idea will help you to remember what any group of letters stands for. ADP stands for adenosine diphosphate. Picture yourself adding up (*add up* will remind you of ADP; or, an *ape* and a *dean* eat *pea*s) all the signs in a den (*add den sign*—adenosine); a diver comes to help and drowns—it's a *diver's fate* (diphosphate).

If you know that, you'll also know that ATP stands for adenosine triphosphate. You can, however, associate it separately if you want to. *A teepee* (ATP) is adding signs in a den, and so on; a *driver's fate* will remind you of triphosphate.

IAA is indole acetic acid. Either a gigantic *eye* voting *"Aye, aye"* or an eye and two apes would remind you of IAA. Associate either one with going into a hole (*in the hole*—indole) to get *a seat* (acetic acid). NAA is napthalene acetic acid. Picture yourself neighing (*neigh*—NAA) as you *nap lean*ing on *a seat*.

DPN is diphosphopyridine nucleotide. Either a *dean* eating a *pea* and a *hen,* or *dippin',* would remind you of DPN. Your picture might be that you're dippin' into the *new clear tide* (nucleotide) and you *die* because a *fast foe* comes *piratin'* out of the water.

Again, I've suggested the first words and pictures that came to my mind; yours might be entirely different, but they'd work just as well. Whether or not you have to remember these groups of letters and what they mean is not important; what is important is that you understand how easy it will be to handle similar memory problems. Letters that have to be memorized in conjunction with something else should never be hard for you after this. To prove it to yourself, why don't you go over the examples again and then see if you remember what the letters mean?

DNA is ....
RNA is ....
ADP is ....
ATP is ....
IAA is ....
NAA is ....
DPN is ....

I recently saw this question on a college biology exam: "Trace a molecule of blood from the heart to the thumb(nail)."

To have answered that question, you would have to have learned (remembered) the path of that molecule when you studied it. A simple Link of Substitute Words will solve that problem. Start with a picture to represent a molecule of blood, perhaps a *mole* that's *cool* and bleeding. Perhaps associate that with *an order* of *airy art* (aorta artery)—the cool and bleeding mole orders art that floats in the air. You could also picture the cool mole coming out of the heart via the large artery, and that would probably be all you'd need.

Associate whatever you're using with a *brake* and a *C fall*-ing into a *trunk* (brachio-cephalic trunk). A *sub* made of *clay* (subclavian artery) comes out of the trunk; a *sick axe* (*axe ill*—axillary artery) wrecks the sub; the axe *breaks* and becomes more *ill* (brachial artery). The pieces of broken axe turn into *radios* (radial artery) or *dials*. The radios have *doors*, which *sail* away on a *pole* and some *ass*es, or donkeys (dorsales pollicis artery).

Remember that I am not studying this subject and am not at all familiar with it. Therefore, I may use reminders for words for which you need no reminders. You may be able to picture the thing itself, without a Substitute Word or thought at all.

Applying the systems is an individual thing; each person will do it just a bit differently. And that's as it should be. The important thing is that the result is the same—learning the material.

25

DISEASES AND VIRUSES

It would help in biology if the student remembered some of the diseases that strike human beings. A couple of fast Links will easily take care of that, and after you have made the Links, you can associate any other information you will need with the name of any disease—facts such as how the disease is spread, its symptoms, its prevention, tests for it, and its treatment.

Suppose you want to remember three protozoan diseases. Start a Link with something to remind you of that heading, perhaps a pro sewin' a toe—*pro toe sewin'*—protozoan. With that, Link *sleeping* (African sleeping sickness); sleeping with *me big D sent Harry* (amebic dysentery); and that with anything that would remind you of malaria. I'd use a mosquito, or you can use *mal* (bad) *air*. Sometimes you can picture the symptom of the disease too, and that, of course, will remind you of the disease itself.

Here are three worm diseases: hookworm, tapeworm, and trichinosis. Start the Link with a picture of a gigantic *worm;* that's the heading. With that, Link a *hook;* the hook is being *taped* to the worm; you're taping someone's *nose* because he does too many *tricks* with it.

Two fungus diseases are athlete's foot and ringworm. Simply picture yourself having *fun* (with *Gus,* if you like) with a large *foot* that has a *ring* on it.

Some bacterial diseases: bubonic plague, diphtheria, pneumonia, tetanus, tuberculosis, typhoid fever, whooping cough, and scarlet fever.

Start your Link with a Substitute Word for bacteria. Perhaps someone's *back* is *tear*ing (being torn or crying). You *blew on it* (close enough to remind you of bubonic; *blue-bonnet* would also do) and then *dipped* something into the *tear.* Whatever you dip in comes out with *new money* in it; this new money is *tied on* an *ass,* which walks *to* an ice*berg* (or *teepee* to remind you of TB). You *tie* a *Ford* to the berg; a gigantic *hoop* flies out of the Ford; the hoop is colored *scarlet,* or has a scar.

Some virus diseases are chicken pox, common cold, influenza, measles, mumps, virus pneumonia, poliomyelitis, rabies (hydrophobia), smallpox, and yellow fever.

Start the Link with *fire* or *wire* (us). A *chicken* is being fired; the chicken is *sneezing* (or *shivering,* if you like). *In flew* many birds who were all sneezing; they were all *spotted.* A bouquet of *mums* was all spotted; *new money* grew out of the mums; the new money is playing *polo* (or *pole my light is*). *Mad dogs* (rabies), or *ray bees,* are playing polo; the mad dogs are running wild in *small parks;* the small parks are all bright *yellow.*

As usual, if you form the Links, see the pictures, and go over them a few times, you'll know the information. After you've done so, add any other information you wish, or form a new Link. For example, you can form a picture of washing a *tied Ford* (typhoid) with *polluted water;* then *carriers* come to carry the Ford away; the carriers eat smelly (*contaminated*) food out of which *flies* appear. Then you'll know how typhoid fever is spread.

To remember additional information, continue the Link—the flies all are hot and have bandages on their heads (fever and headache are the symptoms).

Prevention and test: There's a bandage around the *moon* (immunization); pure water and food falls out of the moon (pure water and food supply); *flies roll* out of the pure water and food (control flies); the flies push carriers away (keep carriers away from foods); the carriers are *all* very *wide* (Widal test). See someone hitting your *toes* with a *strap* because you committed *a sin* and you'll have a reminder that streptomycin is the treatment for typhoid fever.

In biochemistry, it may be necessary for you to know the names and some facts about different viruses. Link *a dinner* (adeno) with *arbor* (arbo) with *her peas* (herpes) with *mixer* (myxo) with *pop over* (papova), and so on, and that will remind you of the names.

You'd probably already know that viruses are measured in millimicrons. If you pictured a girl eating *her peas* (herpes) which came out of *tins* (120), that would remind you that a herpes virus measures about 120 millimicrons in diameter.

Picture a girl whose name is *Dinah* (DNA) coming out of the tins (or use a *dean* with a *hen* and an *ape* on his head; alphabet words for DNA) and you'll know that the herpes virus contains DNA.

Some of the diseases that the herpes virus causes in man are herpes simplex (fever blisters and cold sores), herpes zoster (shingles), salivary diseases, and varicella (chicken pox). Associate whichever name you desire with Dinah; Dinah draws a *simple X* on her *sister* (zoster); the sister *salivates* in a *cellar* (or *where is cellar*—varicella).

26

FOSSIL RACES OF MAN; ORDERS OF MAMMALS; LOWER INVERTEBRATES

Would it be helpful to know the fossil races of man? It's easy enough to do.

JAVA APE MAN (*Pithecanthropus erectus*). An *ape* is sitting at a table drinking *java* (coffee) like a *man*. If you don't know that java is a slang word for coffee, use *javelin* or *"D'ja have a——?"* See this ape trying to throw a pass, but he can't. He throws the ball at you and your friends and "wrecked us," or he's standing erect (*pity he can't throw pass, he wrecked us—Pithecanthropus erectus*). See the picture clearly.

PEKING MAN (*Sinanthropus pekinensis*). Picture a *man peeking* at things. This is a sin and he gets something thrown in his puss. That ends his peekin' (*sin and throw puss, peekin' ends*).

HEIDELBERG MAN (*Homo heidelbergensis*). A man *hides* an ice*berg* in his *home*. The iceberg falls on his sis (sister) and ends (kills) her (*home hide berg end sis*).

NGANGDONG MAN (*Homo soloensis*). A man falls into a pit and *no gang* will go *down* to help him; he's down *so low*, the gangs go *home*.

NEANDERTHAL MAN (*Homo neanderthalensis*). A *knee* and *hand are* very *tall;* the tall knee and hand go *home*.

CRO-MAGNON MAN (*Homo sapiens*). A gigantic *chrome mug* has a *nun* in it. This chrome mug is in your *home* and you're *sippin'* from it.

Form these associations or make your own. Once you've

done that, form a Link to remind you of each one. Start the Link with something that will remind you of fossil races of man. Link java or ape to that; an ape is peekin'; you're peekin' at a hidden (ice)berg. And so on.

After you've formed the Link, you'll know the races and the Latin names. Again, you add whatever you like to the Link. If you want to remember the ages in which the races were on earth, simply make up a word to represent the millions of years and associate that with the race.

The Orders of Mammals

Insectivora (insect-eating animals; shrew, mole, etc.)
Chiroptera (adapted for flight; bat)
Primates (nails instead of claws, among other things; ape, monkey, man)
Edentata (molars without enamel; armadillo, sloth)
Lagomorpha (chisellike incisors, rabbit)
Rodentia (gnawing animals with chisellike incisors; rat, beaver, squirrel)
Carnivora (flesh eaters; cat, dog, wolf)
Cetacea (fish-shaped mammals; dolphin, whale)
Sirenia (aquatic, flipperlike forelimbs; manatee, dugong)
Artiodactyla (even-toed hoofed; deer, camel, pig)
Perissodactyla (odd-toed hoofed; horse, zebra)
Proboscidea (trunk or proboscis; elephant)

To remember the order of mammals, form a Substitute Word or thought for each one and then Link them. Millions of *insect*s (Insectivora) fly into a *chiropractor*'s office (Chiroptera); the chiropractor is treating a gigantic piece of *prime meat* (Primates); the prime meat has *dents* and *holes* in it (Edentata); a *lake of morphine* (Lagomorpha) has many dents and holes; millions of rats (Rodentia) come out of this lake; they go to a *carnival* (Carnivora); the entire carnival is sitting on a gigantic ace (*sit ace*—Cetacea); the ace emits a terribly loud *siren* (Sirenia) sound; some people having *tea on a dock* (Artiodactyla) fall off the dock when they hear the loud siren;

they *perish* near the *dock* (Perissodactyla); an elephant picks them up with its *proboscis* (Proboscidea).

If you want to remember the type of animal that each name signifies, simply form a separate association that will give you that information. For example, a picture of a lake (of morphine) full of millions of chisels will remind you that Lagomorpha is the chisellike incisor group of animals. It would work just as well if the picture were of a lake full of scissors (incisors), or full of rabbits (one of the animals in that category). If one of the "people" having "tea on a dock" were a camel, and if I already knew that camels are even-toed hoofed animals, then I would have the information I need. Anything that reminds you of the information you want to remember can be used in your associations.

Always start your Link with a Substitute Word for the heading; something that will tell you what it is you're remembering. In this case, it has to be a picture that reminds you of "orders of mammals." You might first imagine all the mammals of earth marching in size-place order. Then millions of insects fly out of this orderly parade, and so forth, continuing the Link.

Lower Invertebrates

A similar Link will remind you of the names (or kinds) of some of the obscure lower invertebrates. Start the Link with a "heading" Substitute Word or picture. With that, Link *row too far* (Rotifera); you're *row*ing without *gas*—it's a *trick* (Gastrotricha); you're rowing a *keen orange* (Kinorhyncha) instead of a boat; an *ant* is on *top* of the keen orange holding a *rock* (Entoprocta); the ant tries to throw the rock, but can't, so it falls (*I can't throw so fall*—Acanthocephala). It falls on *no mat* and needs *morphine* (Nematomorpha); the morphine makes it *act* on *top* of a *rock* (Ectoprocta); the entire act on top of the rock is *for Anita* (Phoranidea); Anita *breaks* the *podium* (Brachiopoda); someone on the broken podium *sips on* a pina *colada* (or *cool leader*—Sipunculida); the colada flows down *a corridor* (Echiurida); it is *chas*ing (or *cheat*ing) *a gnat* (Chaetognatha).

If you have to remember the meanings of the words, associate the meaning with the substitute for that particular word. For example, see yourself chasing a gnat with an arrow in your hand to remind you that arrowworms are part of the Chaetognatha class. As you break the podium (Brachiopoda), *lamps* break and *shells* fall out of them (lamp shells are in the Brachiopoda phylum). Associate whatever you want to remember!

27

ERAS, EPOCHS, AND PERIODS OF THE EARTH; ANCIENT PEOPLES AND THEIR CONTRIBUTIONS

When studying the ages of man, you might also find it helpful to be able to remember the eras, epochs, and periods of the earth's history. As usual, you Link what you need to remember, and in the order in which you want to remember it. Again, it's simply a matter of Linking Substitute Words.

The eras are easy; there aren't many of them and they all end in "zoic," so you need remember only the first part of the word. Start your Link with a substitute heading word for era. An eraser would do; you use that to correct an *error*. Or you can use *ear*.

Link that to *ark* and *keyho*le (Archeozoic) or to *ark* or *arch* and donkey (*ass*). Link *ark* to *pro tear O* (Proterozoic); *pro tear O* to *pail* or *pale* (Paleozoic); *pail* to *mess* (Mesozoic); and *mess* to *cent* (Cenozoic).

These are suggestions only; you may not need *pro tear O* to remind you of Proterozoic; just *pro* might do it for you.

Epochs

Do the same thing for the epochs. Start the Link with a Substitute Word for epoch; you can use *he park* or *pocket*. Since each epoch ends with "ocene," you'd merely have to Link your heading to *pleased* or *placed* (Pleistocene); to *ply* or *ploy* (Pliocene); to *me* or *my* (Miocene); to *oh leg* (Oligocene); to *E* or *eel* (Eocene); to *pail* or *pale E* (Paleocene).

If you're really interested in remembering these epochs,

form good clear pictures in your mind, then review the Links once or twice.

Periods

The names for the periods are: Quarternary, Tertiary, Cretaceous, Jurassic, Triassic, Permian, Carboniferous, Devonian, Silurian, Ordovician, Cambrian, and Precambrian.

Start your Link with a Substitute Word for period; I used a dot. Link dot to *quarter,* and you can get *nary* in there, too, if you want to. Either see the quarter floating in the air—it's *airy,* or imagine you have *nary* a *quarter.* Then associate quarter with *thirsty* or *the Hershey airy.*

Link thirsty to *cream taste nauseous* or *gracious;* gracious to *juror sick;* juror to *try a stick;* stick to *purr me in;* purr to *carbon* or *carbon is for us;* carbon to *devil, Dave on,* or *divan* (this one and the rest all end in "ian").

Now Link, say, divan to *silo* or *see lure;* silo to *order fish;* fish to *came by* or *can't be in;* and, finally, came by to *pray came by.*

Form good, clear, ridiculous pictures, then review. You should now know all the eras, epochs, and periods of the earth.

Ancient Peoples and Their Contributions

Short, simple Links will also help you to remember the ancient peoples of the earth and some of their contributions. Here's a list:

EGYPTIANS: metals, calendar, writing, architecture, sculpture, religion, sciences.

SUMERIANS: agriculture, cities, a number system, a unit of measurement.

AKKADIANS AND AMORITES: a more unified government, a better fiscal system, concepts of law and business.

HITTITES: iron tools and weapons.

ASSYRIANS: military science (battering rams, iron-tipped arrows), the first postal system, introduction of cotton crops, sculpture, good highways.

CHALDEANS: imposing architectural monuments, astronomy, astrology.

PERSIANS: a well-governed empire, a pony express, Zoroastrian religion.

PHOENICIANS: navigation, alphabet, trade.

HEBREWS: the Old Testament, dietary laws, the Ten Commandments.

ARAMEANS: land caravans, Semitic writing.

LYDIANS: minted coins.

AEGEAN: seafaring, bronze work, scientific sanitation.

Here now are the fast associations or Links that came to my mind for each of the above:

A pyramid (Egypt) made of metal; a metal calendar; writing on a calendar; a calendar forms a building (architecture); a building is sculpted; a sculpture (statue) goes to church holding some test tubes. Check back and see if you understand why I've used the Substitute Words and thoughts that I have. Form the Link, with your own words if you prefer, and you'll know the information. Do the same with the rest.

Some ears farming (agriculture) in the city (cities); a lot of numbers are in the city (number system); somebody is measuring all the numbers (measurement).

A K dyin' and *a Ma writes* being unified; with fish scales (fiscal); fish scales as lawyers and businessmen.

Hit tights with iron tools and shoot it with a weapon.

A seer iron using battering rams and arrows; arrows delivering mail; mail growing cotton; cotton sculptures; sculptures driving on good highways.

Chilled (or *child*) *iron* forming great architectural monuments; monuments are all over the sky instead of stars (astronomy, astrology).

A *Persian* cat governs an empire; the Empire State Building rides a pony; *Zorro* rides a pony and finds it *a strain,* so he prays.

A *phone* that's *itchin'* navigates a ship; a ship recites the alphabet; people are trading with letters of the alphabet.

A man (*he*) *brews* an *old test* tube; a test tube is on a diet; a man on a diet is eating a stone tablet (Ten Commandments).

Armies (Arameans) are traveling over land in caravans; all the people in the caravans are writing on the *sea* with a *mitt* that *ticks.*

A *lid iron* (iron lid) is lifted and newly minted coins appear.

Aging (*agin'*) men are going to sea; the ships are made of bronze; large chunks of bronze are cleaning the streets (sanitation).

28

CONCEPTS IN SCIENCE AND CHEMISTRY

There are certain concepts in chemistry that must be learned or memorized. For example:

1. When an atom is not neutral, it is an ion.

2. When two atoms are drawn to each other by opposite charges, it is an ionic bond.

3. When electrons are shared, it is a covalent bond.

4. Molecules can be formed only by covalent bond.

5. If there are a different number of neutrons than protons, it is an isotope.

6. Organic molecules contain carbon.

7. Molecules always vibrate.

Simple associations will help you to remember such concepts as these. You should be able to form your own ridiculous pictures by now, pictures that will remind you of what you want to remember, and if you do, you will find the material is already half memorized. However, here's how I memorized the concepts listed above. (Actually, my helping you is not really helping you; when you think up your own words and pictures, the material is already half memorized.)

1. I pictured an atom bomb exploding all over the place (not neutral); it showered *iron* (ion) over everything and everybody.

2. Two atom bombs are being drawn together by a bond; I'm opposed to this so I charge (opposite charge) them, and also *nick* the bond with *iron* (ionic bond).

3. *Electric trains* (electrons) are being shared by children sleeping under a *coverlet* (covalent), which is a large savings bond.

4. A large bond acting as a coverlet has *cool moles* (molecules) forming under it.

5. A lot of *new trains* (neutrons) are eating very little *protein* (protons); the new trains all have *ice on top* (isotope).

6. Some cool moles are playing the organ on a gigantic sheet of carbon paper.

7. The moles are being so cool that they shiver (vibrate) continually.

Each picture was an instantaneous one in my mind, and that was all that was necessary to memorize this information. On your own, apply the same idea to the following material:

1. All matter is composed of particles.
2. The particles of matter are in constant motion.
3. All collisions are perfectly elastic.

The seven crystal systems are: cubic, tetragonal, hexagonal, rhombohedral, rhombic, monoclinic, and triclinic.

If you want to remember them, a simple Link of Substitute Words or thoughts will lock them in for you. For instance, picture an old *crystal* radio set with *cube*s (cubic) flying out of it (or the crystal set is a cube); the cubes turn into neon *tetra*s (tropical fish) and then are *gone*. If you never heard of neon tetras, *dead ray gun* would work as well. The tetras are gone because someone *hexed* them (hexagonal); the hexer is doing a *rhumba* while standing on his *head;* a *Bic* pen does the *rhumba* (rhombic) with him; the Bic pen is injured but refuses to go to a clinic (*no clinic*—monoclinic), but is finally urged to *try* a *clinic* (triclinic).

To give examples of how to apply these systems to all areas of chemistry, biology, physics, and other sciences would take an entire book for each subject. What I am trying to do in the space available is to give you enough different examples so that you'll be able to solve any memory problem. In many instances, knowing the meanings of words will help you grasp the concepts.

Here are some other simple examples:

The important parts of a body cell are the nucleus, cytoplasm, and cell membrane. Picture a prison *cell* full of *new clothes* (nucleus), people *sit*ting on *top* of blood *plasma* (cytoplasm), and *men brains,* or men *rain*ing (membrane).

The five main kinds of compounds in protoplasm are proteins, carbohydrates, fats, minerals, and water. Form a Link: you're taking a *photo* of blood *plasma* (protoplasm); some *teens row* (proteins) over to watch; the teens put *carbon* paper on all the *hydrants* (carbohydrates)—or they're selling carbon paper at *high rates;* the carbon paper is no good, it's dripping with fat; the fat drips all over a *man* on *a rail* (mineral); he dives into water to wash it off.

Remember that I am giving you examples that are completely out of context. Ordinarily, you would apply the systems as you came across the facts in your reading.

If you want to remember the atomic weights and atomic numbers of elements, it should be easy for you now. Beryllium has the atomic weight of 9, and the atomic number of 4. You might see a large, bee (9) *bury*ing a *lily* in a large loaf of rye (4) bread. The larger number is always the atomic weight, so there's no chance of confusing the numbers.

If all you want to remember is the atomic weight, that's the only number you'd associate with the name of the element. As usual, you include what you want to remember. Iodine has the atomic weight of 127. Either see yourself drinking iodine instead of *tonic* (127) or a gigantic *eye* is *din*ing and drinking tonic.

Picture a gigantic tongue (tungsten) being a *diver* to help you remember that the atomic weight of tungsten is 184. Get a *car* into the picture and you'll know that the atomic number is 74.

A large *dish* (16) full of ivy (8) in an *oxygen* tent tells you that oxygen has the atomic weight of 16 and that 8 is the atomic number. (A *dish* of oxygen will also do.) See a thermometer (mercury) in a *nest* (201) making a *fuss* (80), and you'll know the facts about mercury.

What information would this picture give you? A *silly cone* is being cut with a *knife,* and a *tire* rolls out.

If you want to know just the names of the elements, make up Substitute Words and Link them. A Link of: hiding a *row* of *gems* (hydrogen), to *heel* (helium), to *lit* an *E* and an *M* (lithium), to *bury lily* (beryllium), to *boar run* or *moron* (boron), to carbon paper (carbon) tells you the elements with the atomic numbers 1 through 6.

A typical question on a college exam might be: "List in increasing order of atomic number: Na, Cu, F, Au, I, W, Fe, Al, Be, Cs." Therefore, memorizing the atomic numbers will certainly be helpful to you.

Now that you know the alphabet Peg Words, the symbols for the chemical elements are easily handled. The alphabet words and the Substitute Word idea will help you to remember which symbol represents which element.

Many of the symbols are too easy to bother with. I mean those where the letters in the symbol practically tell you the element, such as I = iodine, Br = bromine, F = fluorine. You can, however, apply the systems to any or all of them.

Pb is the symbol for lead. See yourself eating *peas* (P) and *bean*s (B) that are breaking your teeth; they're made of *lead;* or peas and beans are being *led.*

Zr is zirconium. I originally memorized this by picturing a *zebra* (Z) being ridden by a clock (*hour*–R). A large *cone* was coming out of the zebra and I was pointing to it, saying, "*See cone in him.*" If you know that a zircon is a synthetic diamond, you can use *zircon neon*. There's another way to handle the letters, and that is the way you handled formulas. Use a word that would remind you of the letters, for instance, *zero* would remind you of Zr. You can picture a gigantic zero with a *cone in him*. Whatever you use, if you see that picture, it will surely remind you that Zr is zirconium.

You may also have to remember groups of elements. For example, the noble gases are: helium, neon, argon, krypton, xenon, radon. Start a Link with a Substitute Word for *noble,* and continue the Link with either the alphabet word combinations or the Substitute Words for the elements. Using the Substitute Words, the Link might form like this: a nobleman is filling a balloon with *helium;* a balloon is part of a *neon* sign; an *R* is *gone* from a neon sign; Superman, who came from *Krypton* (or *crept on*), puts the *R* back; someone gives him a *Z* to put on the sign, but he says, *"Z? No."* (xenon); he throws the *Z* on a *radio* (radon).

There are other ways to do it, of course; you could have used *heal 'im* for helium, *knee on* for neon, for instance. Or you could have decided to Link the symbols instead of the names; for example, the halogens are F (fluorine), Cl (chlorine), Br (bromine), I (iodine), At (astatine). Perhaps you might picture some *gents* with *halos* (halogens) holding *half* (F) of a piece of *coal* (Cl) out of which comes a *bear* (Br) with one *eye* (I), which the gents *"ate"* (At).

You might want to use this mnemonic aid: A gent with a halo is eating clear broth and saying, *"For clear broth I'd attack."* I don't suggest using this idea often, but used occasionally, it can be helpful.)

Remembering molecular compositions is easy. I use words that remind me of the letters and numbers. H_2 SO_4 is sulfuric acid. The way I originally memorized this was to picture myself pouring sulfuric acid on a hen; this made the *hen sore* (*Hen = H_2, sore = SO_4*). If you need to be reminded of sulfuric, you might use *sold few ricks* as a Substitute phrase. You poured acid on the hen because it sold few ricks (I picture a rickshaw for rick; *rig* or *rag* would do just as well.)

The formula for glucose is $C_6H_{12}O_6$. Cash Hittin' Ouch is what I used to memorize it; *Cash* = C_6, *Hittin'* = H_{12}, *Ouch* = O_6. You can use *glue hose* or *glue coats* to remind you of glucose. So the picture might be: someone is gluing coats together and you hit him with cash (money). He yells, "Ouch!"

29

PHYSICS

In high school and college physics you are required to learn many concepts; applying the systems you've learned will make the chore much easier. Here are some points pertaining to *fission of uranium:*

The product nuclei fly apart in opposite directions with enormous velocities.

The liberation of energy results from the fact that the products have less mass than the original uranium nucleus and neutron combined. Nuclei near the center of the periodic table have less mass per particle than uranium has.

A great variety of product nuclei may be formed.

Since the proportion of neutrons goes up with atomic number, splitting uranium into two elements of lower atomic number results in product nuclei with too many neutrons for stability. The fission products are usually radioactive.

Some of the excess neutrons are freed in the fission process, making a chain reaction possible.

Let us assume you wanted to learn these concepts. You could use the Peg system and learn them by number, or you could Link them. I would use a Link. Start it with a picture that will remind you of the fission of uranium—perhaps, *fishin'* in the *rain*.

If you were applying the systems to this kind of material, you'd have certain standards in a short while. For instance, you might always use *new clay* to represent nuclei and *new train* to represent neutron. After a while just clay and train would suffice. You might use a chocolate bar to represent energy, and so on.

Here's how I might apply the system in order to memorize the concepts listed above. Please remember that just reading doesn't help you learn the material; you must actually see the pictures. And, as usual, you're much better off making up your own words and pictures.

You're fishin' in the rain and *prod*ding some *new clay* (product nuclei) at the same time. The new clay flies apart in opposite directions; the pieces fly with blinding speed, enormous velocities.

These flying pieces of clay free a chocolate bar (liberation of energy); the chocolate bar is liberated because it is smaller (less mass) than the *rain*drops; it is raining *new claws* and *new trains* at the same time (than the original uranium nucleus and neutron combined); this rain is falling on a large table with some new clay at its center (nuclei near the center of the periodic table); the new clay is smaller than each *part* of each raindrop (have less mass per particle than uranium has).

You *prod* the new clay and a great many different-size pieces form (a great variety of product nuclei may be formed).

Some of these pieces form *portions* of new trains (proportion of neutrons) that rise (go up) in an atomic blast (goes up with atomic number); the atomic blast splits a raindrop into two parts; each part falls lower (splitting uranium into two elements of lower atomic number) and prods some new clay (results in product nuclei); many *wobbly* new trains come out of the clay (with too many neutrons for stability); these wobbly trains are *fishin'* and catch moving (active) *radios* (the fission products are usually radioactive).

Some *extra* (new) trains fall out of the radio and form a chain (some of the excess neutrons are freed in the fission process, making a chain reaction possible).

You may do this in an entirely different way. Remember, I am using Substitute Words to remind me of certain words for which you may not need reminders. On the other hand, you may want reminders for words I didn't bother with. As one example, I didn't use anything to remind me of the words "process" and "reaction" in the last concept, but you may think it is necessary.

Two more examples:

Some points pertaining to *controlled chain reaction:*

Some of the neutrons produced by fission escape and cannot contribute any further to the reaction.

When a controlled chain reaction is working at a constant level, each fission supplies, on the average, one neutron which initiates another fission.

Fissions do not consistently form the same fission products. Dozens of different isotopes of intermediate weight have been identified as products of U^{235} fission.

Fission fragments as a rule have too many neutrons for stability and are radioactive. They generally emit beta particles until a stable balance of protons and neutrons is achieved.

These fission fragments accumulate in a reactor, acting as impurities which reduce the efficiency of the chain reactions, so that they must be periodically removed. Disposal of these highly radioactive wastes has been a most troublesome problem.

You're *controlling a chain* while you're fishin', and some new trains come out of the water (some of the neutrons produced by fission); you try to catch the trains, but some escape and refuse to give (contribute) anything to you (escape and cannot contribute any further to the reaction).

Some of these trains (remember, you're Linking the last item of each association with the first item of the next so that one fact will lead you to the next) form a chain that is perfectly straight and controlled (when a controlled chain reaction); the chain remains in midair at a constant level (is working at a constant level); many fishermen appear, and each one supplies one new train for the chain; from each new train, another fisherman appears (each fission supplies one neutron which initiates another fission).

These new fishermen are all fishin', and each one catches different products or fish (fissions do not consistently form the same fission products); some of them catch many pieces of *ice or tape* of intermediate weight (dozens of different isotopes of intermediate weight); these pieces are checked and tagged (or *dent*ed—identified) and prodded onto a *ewe,* an a*nimal* (or *no mule*—U^{235}) which starts fishin' (have been identified as products of U^{235} fission).

The ewe that's fishin' breaks into fragments and too many wobbly new trains loaded with radios come out of it (fission fragments as a rule have too many neutrons for stability and are radioactive); *parts* of the fragments of the ewe leave to place *bets* in a stable where *tons* of new trains are *balanced* (they generally emit beta particles until a stable balance of protons and neutrons is achieved).

The parts of the fragments begin to crowd (accumulate) the stable (you can picture the stable *reacting,* if you like), making the air impure. This causes the new trains to lose their balance and hold on to chains (these fission fragments accumulate in a reactor, acting as impurities which reduce the efficiency of the chain reactions); the fragments are removed and the trains balance efficiently once more (they must be periodically removed); the removed fragments turn into radios, which have loud (high) volume and contain lots of dirt (waste); you try to dispose of them, but it isn't easy, it's quite a problem (disposal of these highly radioactive wastes has been a most troublesome problem).

Three concepts pertaining to *critical mass:*

The chain reaction cannot be maintained unless the proportion of neutrons which escape or are captured is small enough so that those left to continue the reaction average at least one per fission.

The reaction takes place throughout the volume of the material, whereas the escape of neutrons takes place through the surface.

The volume depends on the cube of a dimension; the surface area, on the square.

Picture a *mass of critics* watching a *chain act;* the chain cannot *maintain* its performance, until some *escaped new trains* are made *small enough* and the *remaining* new trains each have at least *one fishin'* pole.

The *acting* chain now recites through a high *volume* speaker as some *new trains escape* from its *surface* only.

The sound (*volume*) is coming out of a *cube* with large *dimensions*; the *surface* on which the chain is standing is a *square*.

Go over the Links I've suggested for controlled chain reaction and critical mass. If you want to remember them, see the pictures and go over the Links a few times. If you don't have to remember this information, you should still go over my suggested Links just to make sure you understand them.

Applying the system to this kind of material is quite similar to the application I'll explain later in the section on remembering as you read. It may seem a bit repetitious to you. However, the application of the systems to this kind of material and to technical reading material is so important that it has to be repetitous. After you've practiced it, and once you thoroughly understand it, the time it will save you will be immeasurable. It may be one of the most useful pieces of learning equipment you'll ever acquire.

A question that appeared on a college physics exam was: "What are Kepler's three laws?" Had you applied my systems to this information when you were originally studying it, answering the question would have been no problem.

Kepler's three laws are:

1. Every planet moves about the sun in an elliptical orbit having the sun at its focus.

2. If a line is drawn from the sun to a planet, it will pass over equal areas in equal intervals of time.

3. The cube of the average orbital radius *R*, divided by the square of its period *T*, is a constant.

I remembered these in 1, 2, 3 order by using tie, Noah, Ma. If you feel you need to be reminded that these are Kepler's laws, simply put a Substitute Word for Kepler into each association; perhaps *cap law, kerplunk,* or *keep low.*

For the first law I pictured ties (1) moving about the sun in elliptical orbits; the sun was always at the center. That's all, but if you see that picture clearly, it should remind you of the law. If you want to, see *caps* being *low* beneath the ties, and you have the reminder that it is one of Kepler's laws.

Second law: A man with a long gray beard (Noah; 2) is drawing a line from the sun to a planet (or *plane,* if you feel you'd rather use a Substitute Word). Picture him doing this (from sun to planet) with other planets at exactly the same time (equal); or if you like, you can picture him drawing the lines with an American flag, the flag to represent equal. You can also see him throwing a *pass* over the same size areas. As usual, you use what you feel will remind you of the material.

Third law: Picture an *average cube*-shaped *radio* in orbit. See it being hit and broken (divided) by a *square* cup of *tea* (T) that has many dots (period) in it. This keeps happening continually, *constantly.*

30

TABLE OF COMMON IONS AND CHARGES; EQUATIONS

A high school student showed me this chart in his textbook and told me that it would be a tremendous help to him if he could memorize the entire thing. The chart is the *table of common ions and their charges* (valences, actually). The periodic table gives you the same information. Here is the chart:

+1	+2	+3
ammonium, NH_4^+	barium, Ba^{++}	aluminum, Al^{+++}
copper (1), Cu^+	calcium, Ca^{++}	chromium (111), Cr^{+++}
mercury (1), Hg_2^{++}	copper (11), Cu^{++}	iron (111), Fe^{+++}
potassium, K^+	iron (11), Fe^{++}	
silver, Ag^+	lead (11), Pb^{++}	
sodium, Na^+	magnesium, Mg^{++}	
	mercury (11), Hg^{++}	
	nickel (11), Ni^{++}	
	zinc, Zn^{++}	

−1	−2	−3
acetate, $C_2H_3O_2^-$	carbonate, $CO_3^=$	phosphate, $PO_4^{\equiv}$
bromide, Br^-	chromate, $CrO_4^=$	
chlorate, Clo_3^-	oxide, $O^=$	
chloride, Cl^-	peroxide, $O_2^=$	
fluoride, F^-	sulfate, $SO_4^=$	
hydrogen carbonate, HCO_3^-	sulfide, $S^=$	
hydrogen sulfate, HSO_4^-	sulfite, $SO_3^=$	
hydroxide, OH^-		
iodide, I^-		
nitrate, NO_3^-		
nitrite, NO_2^-		

There are many ways to apply the memory systems to this problem. I'll tell you how I did it, but you'll still have a few choices to make on your own. Since the charges (+1, +2, −1, etc.) are important, the ions must be associated with them, either by name or by symbol, or both. That's one of the choices you have to make.

The way I worked it out was to use a word that *represented* the charge in each case, and since patterns are easier to remember, I patternized the material, an idea that should be familiar to you because we used it for the vital words of the "memory graph." Let *pl* = *pl*us, and let the next consonant sound represent either 1, 2, or 3. So, +1 can be represented by the word *plate* (*plot*, *plod*, or *Plut*o would also fit the pattern). *Plane* (or·*plan*) can represent only +2 in this pattern, and *plum* (or *plume*) can represent only +3.

Let *mi* = *mi*nus. Using the same pattern, *mite* or *mighty* would represent −1; *mine* or *miner*, −2, and *mime* or *mimic*, −3.

Once you've decided on the words to use, you've made the plus and minus signs, and the digits, tangible. Now they can be pictured. You then have another choice to make; you can associate each ion with the plus or minus word, or you can start a Link with the plus or minus word, then continue the Link with the ions.

Let's use the +2 column as an example. You can start a Link with the plus word, plane. Then associate plane with X ray (drinking barium), or *bar*, or *bah* (to remind you of Ba), or to a bean (B) and an ape (a). Now Link whatever you're using as a Substitute thought for barium to calcium. You can use teeth or bones to represent calcium, or *calls to him,* or a sea (C) with an ape (a) in it. Then Link calcium to copper, copper to iron, and so on.

That's one way. The other way is to associate plane (+2) with barium; then form a separate association of plane with calcium, then plane with copper, plane with iron, etc. You'll have to decide which method is best for you: one straight Link starting with the plus or minus word, or separate associations of the plus or minus word with each ion, or both.

You needn't worry about the plus or minus signs that follow each listed ion, because your plus or minus word tells you how many plus or minus signs belong there. The only exception is the double plus sign beside mercury in the +1 column. This is easy enough to remember because it is an exception but, if you like, you can put something into your original association to remind you of the two plus signs, perhaps two people applauding.

You also don't have to bother with the 1, 11, or 111 in parentheses, although it's simple enough to put, say, bowlegs () into any association to remind you of them. For example, if you're using *I run* as your Substitute Word for iron, and if you picture yourself running with terribly bowed legs, you'll know that parentheses follow the word in the chart. Whether there's a 1, 11, or 111 in the parentheses is no problem, since it's always 1 in the +1 column, 11 in the +2 column, and so on.

All you need do to learn this chart, then, is to decide on the method you want to use and form good, clear pictures. I think you'll be pleasantly surprised at how easily you'll learn the entire table of common ions and their charges.

Equations

Take these same ideas just a bit farther and they'll help you remember similar equations, no matter how long or complicated they may be. The basic equation for photosynthesis is:

$$6CO_2 + 6H_2O \xrightarrow[\text{chlorophyll}]{\text{light}} C_6H_{12}O_6 + 6O_2$$

A Link suggestion: you want to take a photo (photosynthesis) of a cone; it's making noise so you say, *"Sh, cone"* ($6CO_2$); the cone becomes so quiet that you applaud (+); a hen applauds; you hit it with a shoe and it says, "Ow" (*shoe hen ow*—$6H_2O$); the hen yields (the arrow in the equation means yield, as I'm sure you know) and turns light green (light, chlorophyll); it lays some *cash* (C_6), which starts *hittin'* (h_{12}) the hen, who says, "*Ouch* (O_6); the hen applauds (+) again, and you start *chasin'* ($6O_2$) it—or you put *sh*oes o*n* it in order to quiet it.

The same idea will help you memorize the equation for the formation of starch:

$$n\ C_6H_{12}O_6 \longrightarrow (C_6H_{10}O_5)_n + nH_2O$$

Start the Link with anything that will remind you of the formation of starch; a starched collar will do. Link that to *no cash hittin' ouch;* that to arrow; arrow to *cash hits owl;* that to hen applauds; hen applauds to Noah no.

In each of the above, any knowledge you already possess makes the association easier to form, which is so for any association. As one example, you probably know that H_2O is water; in that case, simply use water in the association whenever H_2O appears.

31

CHEMISTRY

The atoms of an element are measured in moles. A mole equals 6.02×10^{13}. It's easy to remember; picture a mole *chasin'* (602) the Sunday *Times* ($\times$) because it was *teasin'* him.

Do you have to remember configurations of elements in your studies? If you do, a Link will make the chore much easier. Scandium has the configuration $1S^2$ $2S^2$ $2P^6$ $3S^2$ $3P^6$ $4S^2$ $3D^1$.

Your Link might go like this: You *scan* a *dime* (scandium); you're *tossin'* ($1S^2$) it into the sun (*in sun*—$2S^2$); it's a *new pitch* ($2P^6$) you're practicing. Associate new pitch with *my son* ($3S^2$), my son with *impish* ($3P^6$), impish with *raisin* ($4S^2$), and raisin with *me dead, my dad,* or *my date* ($3D^1$).

Particles that make up atoms have the following masses:

$$1 \text{ electron} = 9.11 \times 10^{-28}{}_g$$
$$1 \text{ proton} = 1.673 \times 10^{-24}{}_g$$
$$1 \text{ neutron} = 1.675 \times 10^{-24}{}_g$$

You most likely know where the decimal points belong (after the first digit in each of these), where the multiplication sign goes, and that the powers are minus. You also probably know that each one ends with the symbol *g*. What you might need is a reminder for the numbers, and a way to tell which numbers belong to what.

Associate electric train (electron) with *padded tossin' off*.

Associate protein or pro team (proton) with *dash comb designer*.

Associate a fig newton (neutron) with *dish coal designer* (or *to snore*).

Faraday's Constant: 96,487.0 coulombs

Planck's Constant: 6.6256×10^{-27} erg sec

Your Substitute Words for Faraday might be *for* (or four) *a day;* associate that perhaps with some *badger fakes* climbing columns (coulombs). You can put in a word to remind you of constant if you feel it's necessary.

For Planck's Constant you might picture a shoe (6) on a gigantic *plank;* the shoe falls into a *channel* of a*sh* (6256) and reads the Sunday *Times* ($\times$); the Sunday *Times* falls on your toes (10); a *miner* (minus) twists his *neck* (27) looking at your broken toes; you throw an *egg* (erg) a *second* (sec) at him.

One young lady told me that she wanted to remember the critical temperatures for certain gases, because it would help in her chemistry studies. Here is the chart she wanted to memorize:

Gas	Critical Temperature, ° K
H_2	33.3
N_2	126
O_2	154
CO_2	304
SO_2	430
H_2O	647

She memorized the chart in about one minute once she understood the phonetic alphabet and the idea of association. She did it by associating a word that represented the gas with a word or phrase that represented the temperature.

These are the pictures she formed: a hen (H_2) giving its *M*a a *mum*, a nun (N_2) eating a gigantic piece of *Danish* (126) pastry. She pictured herself jumping *on* (O_2) a *tailor* (154), a gigantic ice-cream *cone* (CO_2) counting its money, the ice-cream cone is a *miser* (304). She pictured her son (SO_2) training *rams* (430), a big *O* falling on a hen (*hen O*—H_2O), and the hen emitting a *shriek* (647).

In chemistry, the student is told (at least in the textbooks I've researched) to memorize the names and formulas of the common acids. What could ordinarily be drudgery is almost a game when you apply the memory systems. Here are some common acids and their formulas:

acetic $HC_2H_3O_2$	nitrous HNO_2
boric H_3BO_3	oxalic $H_2C_2O_4$
carbonic H_2CO_3	perchloric $HClO_4$
hydrochloric HCl	phosphoric H_3PO_4
hydrocyanic HCN	sulfuric H_2SO_4
nitric HNO_3	sulfurous H_2SO_3

An association of name with formula is all that's necessary. For the formula, if you can use words or phrases that include the letters and numbers, fine. If you can't, use the alphabet Peg Words for the letters and any phonetically correct words for the numbers.

Form the associations and go over them, and you'll know the formulas for the common acids. One example: *I see* a *tie* hackin' (HC_2) a ham (H_3) to a zone (O_2).

32

STRUCTURAL (CYCLICAL AND CHAIN) FORMULAS

In chemistry and biochemistry you will find it necessary to memorize cyclical structural formulas and straight chain structural formulas. These formulas are difficult to remember for two reasons: there is usually a great deal of similarity of symbols and, also, they form shapes or designs that must be remembered.

Still, applying the systems of association will be extremely helpful. After all, it's when the systems are applied to difficult material that they reveal their real worth; if something is quite easy to remember to begin with, the systems are hardly necessary.

You'll need a few standards. For instance, a word that will always mean *double bond* to you. You can use *bubble* gum, or a two-base hit (double), or just a savings *bond*. Single bonds are usually understood in these formulas, but you can make up a word for that, too. If you need a word for triple bond, you can use *trip* or *ripple*.

Since there are many *O*'s, *C*'s, *H*'s, and *N*'s used in the formulas, you should have good strong pictures to represent those letters. When I memorized them I used a beard (*old*) to represent *O,* a birthday cake (for *age*) to represent *H,* and so on. I've found that these symbols work well. You might want to have a few different words to represent the same letter; *itch, hitch,* and *ache* are fine for *H; open* and *hope* can be used for *O; sea* is the alphabet word for *C,* and you can also use an eye (that you *see* with); *hen* is all right for *N,* and so are *end* and *enemy.*

181

Look at this cyclical structural formula for the pyrimidine thymine:

The first thing to set in your mind is the shape. In this case, simply associate a Substitute Word for thymine with *hexagon* or, if you prefer, with *shoe*, which will tell you that it is a six-sided figure. If the formula you're memorizing is in the shape of a circle, you would associate *circle*. If it's in a square, associate that—or use your Peg Word to tell you how many sides are involved. So, you see, the shape problem is easily solved.

Always start the Link from a definite point on the shape. I'd suggest either eleven or twelve o'clock. If the figure has a definite twelve o'clock point, as this one does, I'd always start at that point, and work clockwise.

Your Link, therefore, might form something like this: You're *ty*ing up a *mine* (thymine) to save it from a *hex* (or a gigantic *X*—hexagon); a gigantic *X* with a long beard (*O*) hits a *double* into the *sea* (double bond, *C*); in the sea *X*'s *chum* (C—CH₃) catches the ball (or *catch 'um* would do); the chum is chewing bubble gum (double bond); a large chunk of bubble gum sneezes (*choo—CH,* or takes a choo choo) and blows over *Noah*, or Noah's ark; Noah *sees trouble* (*C*, double bond) ahead and puts on a beard (*O*) as a disguise; a *hone* (*HN*) falls out of the beard.

You may use either hen or hone to represent *HN*. You may question that. Since hen is the alphabet word for *N*, wouldn't it confuse you and cause you to put an *N* (only) at that point? No, it will not confuse you. Again, don't overlook the essential point. Since applying the system forces Original Awareness, true memory will tell you that *HN*, and not *N*, is written there. Also, it must be assumed that you have some knowledge of the material; that knowledge will tell you that hen represents *HN* here. Of course, you could use hone at both points and avoid the problem. But it really is no problem; try it once and you'll agree.

I've also used double, bubble gum, and trouble to represent double bond. I've done this to show you the different ways you can remind yourself of the same thing. You can do it that way, or use the same standard each time. Instead of a sneeze or a choo choo for *CH*, you could have used a sea with a gigantic birthday cake in it.

One other point: For many formulas I use *hen* to remind me of H_2; here I'm using it to represent *HN*. If you're asking yourself whether or not this would be confusing, I'll give you the same answer as above—it won't. True memory and prior knowledge will tell you the difference. I'm mentioning these things to answer any questions you may have and to show you how pliable the systems are. They can be twisted and manipulated in many different ways.

Go over the Link (either mine or your own), then try to draw the formula. See for yourself how helpful the memory systems are!

This is the straight chain structural formula for pyruvic acid:

$$
\begin{array}{c}
O \\
\parallel \\
C-OH \\
\mid \\
C=O \\
\mid \\
H-C-H \\
\mid \\
H
\end{array}
$$

The problem here is to remember when to go right or left; if not for that it would be a simple straight Link. The problem is easily solved by having a standard to remind you of *right* and a standard to remind you of *left*.

The standards I use for left and right I thought up years ago to help me remember driving instructions: a red flag (Communist, left) for left, and a punch (right cross) for right. Once you've decided on the standards you want to use, this formula becomes a simple straight Link. (Similarly, for straight chain formulas that go from left to right you'd use a standard for *up* and *down*, or *over* and *under*.)

There are many ways to manipulate the memory systems to solve a problem the way you want to solve it. Once you understand the idea you can go ahead and twist it to fit the way your mind works and thinks.

33

ELECTRON DOT SYMBOLS; INTERNATIONAL MORSE CODE

The Lewis electron dot (or electronic) diagrams are designed to show the structure of atoms. I understand that it is not usually necessary to memorize them, although some students have told me they'd like to. Even if it may not be specifically helpful to you, I want to show you how material that might be considered intangible can be made tangible and definite—and therefore easier to remember and learn.

Assume you wanted to remember these symbols: HE:, Li·, Be·, ·B·, ·C·, ·N·, ·O·, :F·, Al,—how would you go about it? You want to know the symbol and where the dots go, and the goal is to make them meaningful. To attain that goal, I've devised a simple pattern; *R* will always equal . (one dot), *T* or *D* will always equal .. or : (two dots), and *S* will always mean *no* dots. Once you have that in mind, the problem is easily solved.

Set a pattern; always start at the top of the symbol, twelve o'clock, and move clockwise. Now one word or phrase associated with the element symbol will tell you the electronic symbol. Using Be. as an example, picture a bee (*B*) stinging an eel (*e*), which is quite *rare* (you can use a *bean* on an *eel*, if you'd rather). The word "rare" tells you where the dots belong (and how many there are). Bee (or bean) and eel tell you the symbol, and since you know that you're starting at the top, rare tells you that one dot goes on top and that the other goes to the right. So it is written Be·.

If you wanted a reminder of the element name also, you could picture a bee flying from a *berry* (beryllium, or *berry ill*) to sting the eel, which is rare.

For He:, the words *sit, sat,* or *sad* would all do. Associate "He" with any one of those words; each starts with an *S*, meaning no dots, and ends with a *T* or *D*, which means two dots. So when you think of "He" your ridiculous picture must remind you that the electronic symbol is He: with no dots on top and two at the right. Include *heel, heel 'em,* or a balloon, and you'll be reminded of the element name, too.

For Li·, associate *lie*—or an *el* train (*L*) with a gigantic *eye* (*i*)—with *sir, sire, sear,* or *sour.* Any of those words, in this pattern, tells you that there's no dot (*S*) on top and one dot (*R*) to the right.

For ·Ḃ·, associate a *bean* (*B*) with *rear sore,* for example. Perhaps you sit on a large bean and it makes your rear sore. "Rear sore" gives you the dot pattern: one dot, one dot, no dot, and one dot, in twelve, three, six, and nine o'clock order.

For ·Ċ·, associate the alphabet Peg Word for *C* (sea) with any word or phrase that contains four *R*'s and no *T*'s or *D*'s; *rarer rye* or *rare roar will do.*

For ·Ṅ:, associate hen (*N*) with *red rower, red rare, rat roar, rod rear, root rower,* etc. Any of these phrases tells you (or reminds you of) the dot formation, one two, one, one.

For ·Ö:, associate old (*O*) with *teeterer.*

For :Ḟ:, associate *half* or effort (*F*) with *tied rat, died root,* or *tight reed.....*

For Ȧ1, associate a man named Al with *rye, rah, row,* etc.

International Morse Code

I'm sure you have the idea now; it's quite simple and works extremely well. While I'm on the subject of dots, I can't resist mentioning the Morse Code. Most likely, you don't have to memorize the code for your studies, but if you did want to do it, the pattern above would fit perfectly. Change it to: *R* = • (dot), *T* (or *D*) = – (dash); that's all you'd need.

The word *rat* (in this pattern) could represent only • —, because it contains an *R* (•) and a *T* (—), in that order. Double *R* and double *T* would mean two of the symbols; for example, for — • • — (X), I use the word *turret*. The words that represent the symbols would have to be associated with the vital letter. I'll mention two methods in a moment. First, here are the letters, their code symbols, and my word suggestions:

A	• —	rat	N	— •	tear (tier)
B	— • • •	terror	O	— — —	touted
C	— • — •	torture (traitor)	P	• — — •	rotator
D	— • •	tearer (dreary)	Q	— — • —	tutored (tethered)
E	•	air (ear)	R	• — •	writer (rotor)
F	• • — •	rear tire	S	• • •	roarer
G	— — •	tighter	T	—	toe
H	• • • •	rarer rye	U	• • —	rarity
I	• •	rower	V	• • • —	re-arrest
J	• — — —	ratted	W	• — —	rated (rooted)
K	— • —	trout (trot)	X	— • • —	turret (tarred)
L	• — • •	retire her	Y	— • — —	treated (traded)
M	— —	toad (tied)	Z	— — • •	teeterer

To remember which word goes with which letter you can simply associate the alphabet Peg Word with the symbol word. Associate ape (*A*) with rat (• —); bean with terror; sea with torture; dean with tearer; eel with air; effort with rear tire; and so on.

Another method is what I call the adjective idea. Make up a phrase, the first word of which (the adjective) begins with the vital letter. The second word is the symbol word. *A*wful rat (*A* • —); *b*ig terror (*B* — • • •); *c*ruel torture (*C* — • — •); *d*reamy tearer (*D* — • •); *e*xcellent air (*E* •); *f*lat rear tire (F • • — •); and on to the end.

There are other ways, but either of the above will serve the purpose admirably. Now, if you want to memorize the International Morse Code, you can do it in minutes. Simply form the associations.

I just wanted to show you that nothing is too abstract to memorize.

34

THE PERIODIC TABLE

When I explained the memory graph I said that the idea could be used to help you remember anything for which it was also necessary to remember location. The graph can be expanded to any size; all you need are words to represent the new squares.

How would you like to memorize the entire periodic table? Even if you wouldn't, I think you should read and study this chapter carefully, because the idea could be of utmost importance for other studies. Once you understand it, you'll be able to memorize a table in a short time. Look at the periodic table in your textbook, and then look at the table on page 189.

If you compare the two you'll see what I've done. I've simply condensed the table by placing the symbols for two elements into all the squares except A1 and G2. The two elements in any square would be written from left to right if you wanted to draw the table. All this will be apparent to you if you compare the table in your textbook with the one shown here.

When you use the same pattern and idea that you used for maps and add to it your knowledge of handling the chemical symbols, you will find that memorizing the entire periodic table becomes fairly easy. There are other ways, of course. You could form separate Links for each row or column of symbols. But I've found the graph to be the easiest way.

To refresh your memory, the vital word for each square must begin with the letter, and the next consonant sound must represent the number. As you can see, the letter is the row and the number is the column. In most cases, I've used a

	1	2	3	4	5	6	7	8	9
A	H								H / He
B	Li / Be						B / C	N / O	F / Ne
C	Na / Mg						Al / Si	P / S	Cl / Ar
D	K / Ca	Sc / Ti	V / Cr	Mn / Fe	Co / Ni	Cu / Zn	Ga / Ge	As / Se	Br / Kr
E	Rb / Sr	Y / Zr	Nb / Mo	Tc / Ru	Rh / Pd	Ag / Cd	In / Sn	Sb / Te	I / Xe
F	Cs / Ba	La / Hf	Ta / W	Re / Os	Ir / Pt	Au / Hg	Tl / Pb	Bi / Po	At / Rn
G	Fr / Ra	Ac							
H			Ce / Pr	Nd / Pm	Sm / Eu	Gd / Tb	Dy / Ho	Er / Tm	Yb / Lu
I			Th / Pa	U / Np	Pu / Am	Cm / Bk	Cf / Es	Fm / Md	No / Lw

word that ends with that consonant sound, but there are a few exceptions. For E3, I use *em*peror. Since we're interested only in the consonant sound that follows the first letter, simply disregard the sounds that come after that. For this pattern, *em*peror could stand only for E3, and vice versa. Another exception is I9; it's the only one where the word begins with a letter other than the vital one. But since *Y* is not used here, you'd know that *yipe* represents I9. However, don't worry about these exceptions; they're easier to remember *because* they're exceptions.

Here are the vital words for the necessary squares, the symbols, and a suggestion or two for words to use to remind you of the symbols.

A1; ate—(H) age or ache
A9; ape—(H;He) itch he or he he

B1; bat—(Li;Be) liberty
B7; bug—(B;C) Before Christ or Bic
B8; buff—(N;O) no
B9; baby—(F;Ne) fine

C1; cat—(Na;Mg) nay mug
C7; coke—(Al;Si) Al, si (yes)
C8; cave—(P;S) PS, pose
C9; cap—(Cl;Ar) Clara, clear

D1; dot—(K;Ca) cane cave, cane cake
D2; den—(Sc;Ti) scat eye, sic Ty
D3; dam—(V;Cr) vicar
D4; deer—(Mn;Fe) man fee, my knife
D5; doll—(Co;Ni) coney, cold night
D6; dash—(Cu;Zn) cousin, cue zone
D7; dog—(Ga;Ge) gauge, Georgia, gee

D8; dive—(As;Se) asset
D9; dope—(Br;Kr) broker

E1; eddy—(Rb;Sr) rib sore
E2; enter—(Y;Zr) yezzir, wine zero
E3; emperor—(Nb;Mo) nab Moe
E4; err—(Tc;Ru) tic Ruth
E5; eel—(Rh;Pd) blood police department (or paid)
E6; edge—(Ag;Cd) age cod (or cad)
E7; egg—(In;Sn) in sun, insane
E8; eve—(Sb;Te) sub team (or tea)
E9; ebb—(I;Xe) eye (or I) Xerox

F1; fat—(Cs;Ba) Casbah
F2; fun—(La;Hf) lay hi-fi, lay half
F3; foam—(Ta;W) Taiwan, ta-ta, Waterloo, tawny
F4; fur—(Re;Os) Renos, re: Oscar
F5; foil—(Ir;Pt) ire pot, iron pot

F6; fish–(Au;Hg) hey you hag
(or hog), autumn hog
F7; fake–(Tl;Pb) tall pub
F8; fife–(Bi;Po) buy (or bi)
pole
F9; fib–(At;Rn) a train, a turn,
a Registered Nurse

G1; gat–(Fr;Ra) fire ray
G2; gown–(Ac) ace, act, AC
current

H3; ham–(Ce;Pr) cent per, ice
prongs
H4; hare–(Nd;Pm) nod PM
H5; hill–(Sm;Eu) small ewe,
some eulogy
H6; hash–(Gd;Tb) good Tab,
good TB
H7; hog–(Dy;Ho) dye hole
H8; hive–(Er;Tm) ear time
H9; hop–(Yb;Lu) wine blue

I3; I'm–(Th;Pa) the Pa
I4; ire–(U;Np) you nap, UN pea
I5; ill–(Pu;Am) pew AM
I6; itch–(Cm;Bk) come book (or back)
I7; icky–(Cf;Es) cafés, café espresso
I8; ivy–(Fm;Md) FM doctor, famous doctor
I9; (y)ipe–(No;Ln) no line

If you've gone over the list of words and symbols it all should be clear to you. The suggestions I've given for the symbol reminders are the first things that came to my mind and the ones that I, personally, would use. Remember that they are meant only to be reminders and need not be exact. I've used the alphabet words here and there; you can use them more often, if you like. For example, for H5 the symbols are Sm and Eu. You could picture an ess curve (S) with a ham (m) driving on it, going up a hill (H5); an eel (E) and a ewe (u) are sitting on the ham. That association would make it definite; I just find it easier to use the kind of reminders listed above.

A funeral taking place on a hill and the eulogy going on and on, which makes me think, "Some eulogy," is all I really need to be reminded that Sm and Eu go into square H5—or next to each other if I'm laying out the periodic table. For F6, associating *aw heck* with fish would be enough to remind me that Au and Hg belong there, even though the phrase contains different letters.

I'd suggest that you learn all the vital words first; that should take very little time if you know the phonetic alphabet. Once you're familiar with them, make each association of vital word with the word or phrase that tells you the symbol.

Here are just a few suggestions for the associations: For E5, you could picture an *eel* bleeding; his blood is *RH* factor and the police department (PD) comes to investigate.

F1: a *fat* man is walking in the Casbah (Cs;Ba). C1: a *cat* is being offered a mug of something; it says "Nay" to the mug (Na;Mg). I5: you're very *ill* as you go to church and sit in a pew in the AM (Pu;AM). D7: a *dog* lands in Georgia and says, "Georgia, gee!" (Ga;Ge). B8: someone wants to *buff* your shoes or fingernails, but you say "No" (N;O); a hen (N) saying "Oh" (O) would also do. A9: an *ape* is laughing, he, he (H;He). G1: you have a *"gat"* that fires a ray (Fr;Ra). H3: you're buying a *ham* at so many cents per (Ce;Pr) pound, or you're picking up a ham with ice prongs. (If you are afraid *ham* will confuse you with ham for *M,* although it won't, you can use *home* as the word for H3.) 17: you go into a few cafés (Cf;Es); they're all *"icky."*

And so on. I think you have the idea now. You can change any words you want to change, as long as the vital word you use fits the pattern, and as long as the words you use for the symbols remind *you* of the symbols.

If you prefer to use a Substitute Word for the element itself, it will work just as well. For square F4, you can picture a gigantic *fur* coat writing a letter, which starts, *"Re: Os*car"; that would tell you that Re and Os go into that area or square. But if you'd rather, you can associate fur with, say, *rainy* (rhenium) and *'at's me* or *ask me* (osmium).

Once you have made all of the associations, all you have to do is lay out a 9×9 graph (or picture it in your mind), and think of your vital words. When you think of E5 (eel), that will tell you that Rh and Pd belong there. Think of D5 (doll) and you'll know that Co and Ni belong directly above Rh and Pd. Think of F5 (foil) and you'll know that Ir and Pt belong directly below, and so on.

If rows H and I are not important to you, just omit them; then your graph would go from A1 to G2. I've given you the vital words for only the squares that are used.

You can expand the graph to ten or eleven columns; lay it out any way you like. I mention this just in case you'd rather not double up the symbols in the first and/or last columns. If you expand to eleven columns, you'll need vital words for A10 and A11 up to I10 and I11. They are easy enough to find; just stay within the pattern. For the 10's, use the *S* sound only; *ace* would represent A10; *base,* B10, etc. For A11, you can use *added;* B11, *bated;* C11, *coated;* D11, *dated;* E11, *edit;* F11, *feted* or *faded;* H11, *hated;* and I11, *I dead.*

Well, there you have it. Using this system, eleven- and twelve-year-old students have memorized the entire periodic table in about half an hour!

Keep in mind that you can put any other information into the original association. Perhaps you want to remember the atomic numbers of each element; you can do it as explained a few chapters ago, or you can simply put a word that tells you the number into the original association for the graph. Yttrium (Y) and zirconium (Zr) are in square E2. Your original picture may have been that you're asking someone to enter (E2) your home and you're saying, "Yezzir" (yes, sir), or that *a tree* (yttrium) with a *cone on 'im* (zirconium) is entering your home. In either case, simply get, say, *moppers* (3940) into the picture. It will tell you that these two elements have the atomic numbers of 39 and 40, respectively.

It's actually easier than that. Since the elements in a square have ascending atomic numbers, all you really need in the above association is *mop* because you'd know that the other symbol's atomic number is one higher, or 40. Then, in your association for F1 include a *lily* (55). It will tell you that the atomic number for Cs (cesium) is 55 and that the atomic number for Ba (barium) is 56, one higher. Add one more word or phrase to your original association and you can have a reminder for the atomic weight as well.

An eddy (E1) is a whirlpool. Your original association might be that you fall into an eddy and a rib (Rb) gets hurt and sore (Sr), or, if you're using the element names, that a ruby (rubidium) falls into an eddy and uses all its strength (strontium) to get out. If you get a *mug* (37) into the picture, that will tell you that rubidium's atomic number is 37, and that strontium's is 38. If you also include, say, *fuller cow* (85.47) and *faction* or *fiction* (87.62), you'll know the atomic weights.

Of course it will take a bit longer to make up the words and to form the associations if you want to include atomic numbers and weights, but you'll also be memorizing that much more information. It would take you longer to memorize more information whether you used a system or not.

35

MEDICAL TERMINOLOGY

If you intend to study medicine and anatomy, or already are, you will be required to learn the names of the parts of the body. The Substitute Word system in conjunction with the Link system will make this learning easier. You might look at a diagram of the human skeleton and decide to remember the names of the bones from the head down. Here are some of the names as an example:

head: frontal, malar, maxilla, mandible
shoulder: clavicle
spinal column: cervical vertebrae, lumbar vertebrae
chest: sternum
pelvis: sacrum
arm: humerus, ulna, radius
hand: carpus, phalanges
leg: femur, patella, tibia, fibula
foot: tarsus, phalanges

Start the Link with a picture of a skeleton. The skeleton is facing *front* and is very *tall* (frontal); someone with a tall front keeps mailing letters—he's a *mailer* (malar); a *Mack* truck is mailing letters; it gets *ill a*s it does so (*Mack's ill*—maxilla).

Someone who is ill has to *man the bull* (mandible) in the bullring; the bull starts to *claw* at a *vehicle* (clavicle); then the bull serves the vehicle a cold meal (*serve a cold*—cervical vertebrae); a gigantic piece of *lumber* (lumbar vertebrae) starts to eat the cold meal; it eats a *ham* that's very *stern* (sternum); a stern ham is holding a *sack* full of *rum* (sacrum); people see the sack of rum, think it's *humorous* (humerus), and laugh.

The sack of rum attacks the laughing people, and they scream,

"Oh, no" (ulna); many *radios* (radius) scream, "Oh, no"; millions of *carpets* (carpus) fly out of the radios; some carpets can swim in anything but juice—they always *fail in juice* (phalanges); a glass of juice pays *more* of a *fee* (femur); someone pays a fee to *pat Ella,* or *pat teller, Pa teller, Pa tell her* (patella); the person paying the fee has *TB,* or *tippier,* tuba (tibia); the person with TB tells a *fib* to *you,* and you're the *law* (fibula); the person telling the fib asks someone to *tar* (*tar* and feather) *us* (tarsus); there's tar all over your toes (phalanges), or use *fail in juice* again.

You can use the Peg system to learn the bones by number, but I see no reason for that. Go over the Link once or twice, add all the bones you want to remember and you'll know them all. Of course, at the same time you can include other information in the Link.

The bones on one side of the pelvic appendage are: one femur, one patella, one tibia, one fibula, seven tarsals, five metatarsals, and fourteen phalanges. If it is important for you to know that, you can make this kind of Link:

Start with something that represents pelvic appendage; perhaps a pail with a wick in it (*pail wick*) and a tail (appendage) on the outside. Associate that with *fee more;* fee more with *pat Ella;* pat Ella with *TB;* TB with *fib you law.* There is one of each.

Then associate fib you law with cow (7) *tar sails.* Perhaps a cow, dressed as a policeman, is fibbing and tarring sails. That will remind you of both the name of the bone and the number—seven, in this case.

To avoid confusion, don't use law for 5 when you continue the Link. You can use any word that has the *L* sound only. *Hill* would do, or use the alphabet Peg Word for 5, which is *eel.* (It would represent 5 phonetically also, since it, too, has only one consonant sound—*L.*)

Your next picture might be that of an eel meeting (shaking hands with) a sail covered with tar (*met a tar sail*—metatarsals). Finally, you shake hands with a tire (14) and the tire *falls in juice* (phalanges).

This fast Link will put the information you wanted right at your fingertips.

Some of the sections of the human brain are the cerebrum, cerebellum, medulla oblongata and pons, and diencephalon. If you are already familiar with them and just need simple reminders, a Link of *broom* to *bell* to *dull* (or *long*) to *puns* (or *pans*) to *surf alone* would do it.

If you're not that familiar with them, simply use Substitute Words that give you more of the sounds. For example: *Sarah broom* for cerebrum, *dyin' to surf alone* for diencephalon, and so on. In either case, start the Link with a picture that will remind you of *brain*.

If you think you know the names of the sections and just want to be reminded of them, you can use a sentence such as, *My Pretty Cousin Digs Cake*, or *Carrying Cargo Makes Pants Dirty*. Be sure that you associate the sentence with *brain*. It won't do much good to know the sentence if you don't know what it represents.

Medical students use many such mnemonic devices to help them remember what they are studying. One fairly well-known mnemonic is:

> *On Old Olympia's Towering Top*
> *A Finn And German Vault And Hop.*

It is used to help a student remember the cranial nerves: optic, olfactory, oculomotor, trochlear, trigeminal, abducens, facial, auditory, glossopharyngeal, vagus, accessory, hypoglossal.

Using a word, phrase, sentence, or rhyme as a mnemonic, or memory, aid is nothing new. The problem, of course, is that a device that helps you to remember the first letters of study material doesn't necessarily help you remember the words themselves. A Link of Substitute Words will help you do that easily. Start the Link with, say, a picture of a *crane* with a lot of *nerve*. See that crane ticking and floating upward (*up tick*—optic).

Optic to olfactory: see an *old* decrepit *factory* ticking loudly as it floats up.

Olfactory to oculomotor: picture the old factory being run by *a cool motor*.

Oculomotor to trochlear: a cool motor is being *thrown clear*.

Trochlear to trigeminal: you try on a gem (or *try gem on Al*), then throw it clear (or *clear* your *throat*).

Trigeminal to abducens: you try on a gem but realize that all you have is two cents (*have two cents*—abducens).

Abducens to facial: all you have is two cents, but it's enough to get a *facial*.

Facial to auditory: you're getting a facial in an *auditorium*.

Auditory to glossopharyngeal: an auditorium is being used as a jail for a glossy (see him shining) pharaoh (*glossy pharaoh in jail*—glossopharyngeal).

Glossopharyngeal to vague: the glossy pharaoh (in jail) is disappearing; he's growing *vague*.

Vagus to accessory: an *accessory* that you're using grows vague (disappears) as you use it.

Accessory to hypoglossal: you're using a gigantic *glossy hypo*dermic needle as an accessory.

Form this Link, and you'll know all the cranial nerves. Obviously, you can remember the meaning of any of the words, if you want to. To remember that olfactory means *pertaining to smell,* simply picture an old factory that smells terrible, that's all.

You may prefer to use the Peg system for the cranial nerves. I've been told by medical and dental students that these nerves should be known by number. Applying the Peg system takes care of that admirably; simply associate the Substitute Word or phrase with your basic Peg Word. An association of a cow (7) getting a facial would tell you that the facial nerve is the seventh cranial nerve. See a policeman (law, 5) trying on a gem, and you'll know that the trigeminal nerve is the fifth cranial nerve. Picture a glossy sheet of tin (12) getting, or giving, a hypodermic injection, and you'll know that hypoglossal is the twelfth cranial nerve.

One of my students, who is also a dental student, told me that he learned the names of the amino acids easily and in almost no time at all by applying the Substitute Word and Link systems. (You can use the Peg system, if you like. Even though you don't have to know the acids in and out of order, by number, some peoples feel that it is more definite to learn them that way. That is up to you.) Here are the acids:

alanine	phenylalanine	histidine
glycine	tyrosine	lysine
valine	serine	aspartic acid
leucine	threonine	glutamic acid
isoleucine	methionine	hydroxyproline
proline	arginine	hydroxylysine

Since the student knew which acids ended in "ine" or "nine," he didn't bother with those endings. He Linked the following Substitute Words or thoughts (the words in parentheses are words I might have used):

A man named *Alan* to *gloss* (*glossy, listen*), to *valet* (*valley*), to *loose* (*loosen*), to *I sew loose* (*ice loose*), to *pro* (*prowl*), to *fanning an E* as you sing "*La la*" (*Fanny la la*), to *Taurus* (*tyros, tie rows*), to *serene* (*sir*), to *three O*'s, to *method, to aw gee* (*archin'*), to *history* (*his tie dine*), to *lies* or *lye,* to *a spare tick* (*us part*), to *glue atomic,* to *hide rocks see pro* (*hide Roxy pro, hide rock zebra*), to *hide* (more) *rocks see lie.*

The ridiculous pictures themselves should come pretty easily now, and let me remind you that you should not think of this as "too much work." Of course it's work, but much less work than if you had to memorize the information by rote without any system. Applying the memory systems is the *easy* way, besides being a challenge, fun, and a way of forcing you to use your imagination. Most important, applying the systems forces you to concentrate on the new information.

You might read something like the following in a college text on histology:

The circulatory system consists of a blood vascular system and a lymph vascular system. The blood vascular system consists of 1) the heart, which is a pump for propelling the blood, 2) the arteries, which are tubes for conveying the blood toward the organs and tissues, 3) the capillaries, which provide for interchange of substances between the blood and tissue fluids, and 4) the veins which serve for the return of blood to the heart.

The lymph vascular system consists of lymphatic capillaries and various sized lymphatic vessels which ultimately drain into two main trunks—the thoracic duct and the right lymphatic duct, which empty into large veins in the neck.

When I think of the word "system," I think of gamblers using a system in order to win at the roulette wheel. Picture the wheel going around in circles. That will remind you of *circulatory system;* or simply picture blood coursing through a body. With whatever you're using, associate blood spurting out and changing color fast (*fast color*—vascular); *vast cooler* would also do. Someone *limps* (lymph) out of the blood, also changing color fast. The foregoing gives you the main piece of information—the circulatory system consists of a blood vascular system and a lymph vascular system. If you need to be reminded of the word *system* in each case, simply stick in a word to remind you of it, although I doubt if that's necessary.

Now form a Link starting with the spurting blood that's

changing color fast. With that, associate anything that will remind you of heart, either the organ itself, a Valentine card, or hearth. With it, associate a word that will remind you of arteries (*I tear E's, harder E's, are there E's,* for example.)

Arteries must lead you to capillaries, so associate whatever you're using for arteries with *cap ill* or *cap ill air.* With that, associate a word that will remind you of veins (varicose veins or vines). That's it. If you need to be reminded of the functions, you can do that too. For instance, associate heart (or whatever Substitute Word you're using) with pump for propelling the blood.

Now form a separate Link for the lymph vascular system. The limping man who's changing color fast is wearing a *cap* that limps off his head (lymphatic capillaries); different or various sized boats (*vessels*) limp out of the cap (lymphatic vessels); all these limping things go into two large trunks (ultimately drain into two main trunks). If you wanted to remember that they *drain* into two main trunks, you could have pictured the limping things going into a *train* first. You can make any association as definite as you want it to be.

See one trunk being *sore* and *sick* (thoracic), or imagine that it contains a *(duck)* (duct) that's sore and sick, and that the other trunk contains a *limping duck* that you hit with a *right* cross (right lymphatic duct) to the neck. Two large veins come out of its neck (empty into two large veins in the neck).

I've used the first things that came to my mind. Even with no knowledge of the subject, I've memorized it as I've written it. If you're studying the material, then you can actually picture some of the things, and you won't need Substitute Words. Use whatever works for you. And obviously, it is always easier when you apply the system to material with which you have some familiarity.

With but a little practice (that is, using the systems) you'll be able to memorize something like this *as you read it*. And even if it forces you to read slower than usual, you'll still be saving time because you won't have to read it over and over again. Most important, once you've applied this system to the material, you'll know that material for as long as you need to know it! Go over "the circulatory system," form the Links and really see the pictures, and you'll see that this is so.

Although there are other ways to apply the systems to this kind of material (the memory graph is one), a Link would suffice in this case. Assume you looked at a diagram that depicted the dissection of the right ear, and that you'd like to memorize it.

Start at any point and form a Link going clockwise. Here's what the diagram might look like, starting at eleven o'clock:

prominence of lateral semicircular canal in aditus to mastoid antrum; posterior and anterior semicircular canals; geniculate ganglion of facial nerve; spiral ganglion of cochlea; vestibular nerve; cochlear nerve; internal acoustic meatus; scala tympani; cochlear duct; scala vestibuli and osseous spiral lamina of cochlea; helicotrema; processus cochleariformis; tympanic membrane; auditory tube; promontory; handle of malleus; stapes; incus.

Assuming you have some familiarity with what you're studying, all you need are simple Subsitute Words to remind you of each part; probably much simpler than the ones I'll suggest.

A man at a *prom* throws a *lateral* pass across a *canal* with a *semicircular* ball; it *adds* itself to a *mass* of *ants,* or *ants* drinking *rum* (prominence of lateral semicircular canal in aditus to mastoid antrum).

From the mass of ants grows a *post* with an *ant ear* on it, the ear falls into a *semicircular canal* (posterior and anterior semicircular canals).

A girl named *Jenny,* carrying a *cue* stick, swims out of this canal. A *gang* of *lions* (or a *gangly* man) follows her; all the lions have tremendous *faces* with twitching *nerves* (geniculate ganglion of facial nerve).

The gang of lions falls, *spirals,* into a meadow (*lea*) full of roosters (*cock*) (spiral ganglion of cochlea).

One of the roosters is named *Beulah* and wears a *vest,* or one of the roosters enters a *vestibule* (vestibular nerve).

The rooster with the vest *lears* at another *cock* (cochlear nerve).

This other cock is an *interne* who holds *a cue stick* and runs to *meet us* (internal acoustic meatus).

The cock with the cue stick *scales* a gigantic *tin pan* (scala tympani).

The tin pan sheds ducks all over the *lea* of *cocks* (cochlear duct).

Some of these ducks *scale* a *vest* (or vestibule) and shout *"Oh, see us"* and then fall (*spirals*) and *lam in the lea of cocks* (scala vestibuli and osseous spiral lamina of cochlea).

The ducks lam to a *helicopter* that's in a *tree* (helicotrema).

The helicopter is in the *process* of *form*ing itself into a *cock* that *leers* (processus cochleariformis).

Then it flies into a gigantic *tin pan* (tympani membrane).

A large *tube* comes out of the tin pan and sits in an *auditorium* (auditory tube).

The auditorium is on a *promontory* of land (promontory).

A girl named *Alice* (malleus; or *mail us*) picks up this promontory by a gigantic *handle* (handle of malleus).

This handle is *stapled* down by some *Incas* (stapes; incus).

As usual, it takes much longer for me to write and explain the pictures than it takes to form them. Go over the Link once or twice, and "lock in" the information.

36

BASIC COLLEGE PSYCHOLOGY

One of the questions I saw on an exam in basic college psychology was this: "List and explain three primary and four secondary defense mechanisms."

Now obviously, after a while, you should know and recognize the defense mechanisms almost immediately, but at first, they must be memorized. If nothing else, memorizing information will help you pass your exams, which, in most instances, do nothing more than test your memory!

To memorize the defense mechanisms you have to decide which method is best for you. You can use the Peg method and remember them by number, or Link them in the order you desire. You can use your basic Peg Words for the secondary defense mechanisms, since there are more of them, and any alternate Peg Words to represent numbers 1, 2, and 3 for the primary defense mechanisms. However, if you used tie, Noah, Ma for the primary, and then used them again for the secondary, you'd probably still memorize them correctly. It's up to you.

Using the alphabet Peg Words for the primary defense mechanisms, associate ape (1) with *denial*. You're arguing with an ape and all you get are denials. That's the first picture that comes to my mind. You use whatever you like, as long as ape reminds you of denial. Be sure to see the picture.

Bean (2) with *repression*. You've just pressed (ironed) a gigantic bean, but it's still all wrinkled, so you re-press it.

Sea (3) with *isolation*. You're isolated in a vast sea.

The secondary defense mechanisms are 1) displacement, 2) projection, 3) identification, 4) rationalization, 5) intellectualization, 6) substitution, 7) fantasy, 8) regression. Using the basic Peg Words, I had these as my first thoughts:

My tie (1) is around my chest instead of my neck; it's been *displaced*.

Noah (2) is showing a movie on the ark; he's the *projectionist*.

My Ma (3) is hanging from my wrist; she's my *identification* bracelet.

I'm giving people small pieces of my rye (4) bread; I'm *rationing* it.

A policeman (law, 5) is discussing a crime with a dangerous criminal; he's *intellectualizing* instead of acting and arresting the man.

I'm putting other things on my feet instead of shoes (6); I'm *substituting* other things for them.

A cow (7) is lying in a field and *fantasizing*—having dreams.

A large quantity of ivy (8) is walking, or moving, backward; it's *regressing*.

The examination question also asked the student to explain the mechanisms listed. To remember the meanings use the Substitute Word idea. You can do that first and then Link or Peg the mechanisms, or do it afterward. The best way would be to do it at the same time. For instance, when you form your association between law and intellectualization, get a reminder of the meaning into the picture at the same time.

The policeman is discussing the crime because he's *retreating from the world of impulse and affect to the world of words and abstractions*. If you want to remember exact words, put anything that would remind you of them into the picture, such as pulse to remind you of impulse. Perhaps the policeman is taking his pulse as he intellectualizes. Extract can remind you of abstract.

Sea and isolation: You're isolated in a vast sea, but then

ideas and feelings that belong together start to appear; you keep them apart.

The ivy regresses; it keeps moving backward until it is far away; it has avoided the anxiety of whether or not it can grow to the top of the fence.

I think you have the idea now. To save you looking them up, here are the descriptions of the defense mechanisms:

Denial: refusal to recognize painful percepts, thoughts, or feelings.

Repression: total inhibition of affect or idea.

Isolation: keeping apart ideas and/or feelings that belong together.

Displacement: substituting for a goal object to fulfill a normal emotion.

Projection: attributing objectionable internal ideas or feelings onto others.

Identification: acquiring a desired characteristic by equating oneself with the ego of another.

Rationalization: offering plausible causal content for unconscious true reason.

Intellectualization: retreat from world of impulse and affect to world of words and abstractions.

Substitution: substituting one act for another that has caused anxiety.

Fantasy: imagining the satisfaction of frustrated motives.

Regression: avoidance of anxiety by reverting to age-inappropriate behavior.

Applying the system actually simplifies the work. As I'll discuss in the chapters on reading, the system forces you (and helps you) to boil down hundreds or thousands of complicated words to a few simple words or thoughts.

One student asked me to help him remember these points pertaining to the *scientific method of observation:*

1. Collect the facts by making systematic observations and recording these facts.

2. Evaluate the data (recorded observations).

3. Communicate the results and conclusions to others.

4. Add the discoveries to other (existing) solutions.

5. Provide the next investigator with a more advantageous starting point.

I've already simplified the material; the wording in the textbook is more voluminous and complicated. Since you're studying this subject, all you need are reminders. In any stated fact there is always one main, or *key,* thought (or word) that will remind you of the entire thought.

When I think of "scientist," I picture a gigantic test tube. If I see that test tube observing things systematically, I have the start of a Link. I might see that test tube *collecting records* (the kind you put on a record player) as it's observing; it is stacking the good records in one pile and the bad ones in another (*evaluating*). I'd picture the two stacks of records talking (*communicating*) to each other. These talking record stacks grow higher and higher as someone *adds* records to them (see them growing as tall as a building). The two tall stacks of records then go out and *provide help* for other record stacks.

Do you see how applying the system, forming this Link, has simplified as it helped you remember? Within the context of the subject, *communicate* could mean only communicating the results and conclusions to others. The one word, and one picture, will bring all that to mind.

Just one more example: In the study of Freudian psychology you may want to remember that *compensation* means "covering up weaknesses by enlarging a desirable trait, or making up for frustration in one area by overgratification in another."

I realize that using one example like this seems easy and obvious—what else would compensation mean within this context? But I also realize, as you should, that when there are many of these meanings to learn, it can become a chore.

The picture I formed to help remember this was instantaneous. I've finished some work and I approach the boss to be *compensated* (paid); one side of my body is ugly, so I approach with the other side toward him; this good side grows much larger (enlarges) than the ugly side. That's all. This association will remind me of the entire thought. There are many more examples of how to solve this kind of memory problem in the following chapters.

37

HOW TO REMEMBER
WHAT YOU READ; LISTENING

All through school—and life—it will be necessary for you to read and gather information, particularly now, living as we do in the age of the "information explosion." One way to accumulate information as you read is to associate and remember the items that you feel are important as you come to them. You simply do as you have already done. Only now, after a bit of practice, you'll be able to do it while you are reading. Simply Link Substitute Words.

Perhaps you'd like to remember some facts in sequence as you read. You should first read the material to make sure you really want to remember it and also to get the gist of it. In that way, you'll have an overall picture of what you want to remember.

Then read it again, applying the memory systems as you go along to lock in the important facts.

I've selected the following as one example. Assume that you want to remember it, and then read it over once.

GREECE

Across the Mediterranean Sea from Egypt is a rocky peninsula with an uneven coast. This is the mainland of Greece. East of the peninsula, in the Aegean Sea, are lots of islands, some large and some small. These lands were the home of Greek civilization.

The first Greeks probably came to the region about 2000 B.C. By 1500 B.C., some of them had a civilization. They knew how to write and paint, and they built great palaces. But they spent most of their time fighting. About 1100 B.C., they were conquered by other Greek tribes who were not so civilized.

Next, all you have to do is to form a Link of the important (to you) facts. Start the Link with a Substitute Word for the heading, Greece. Headings are important; they usually give you the important points of the subject. In most cases, all you have to do is to Link the essential points starting with the heading, as we'll do with this example. In other cases, just Linking the headings themselves will help you to memorize the important information in a chapter or book. I've just mentioned this fleetingly, but don't overlook it. It is possible for you to go through a book once, and know all the main points in sequence, simply by Linking the headings (chapter headings, or bold type).

All right then. If you have read the excerpt once, with concentration, go over it again and form the Link. A test on the information comes later.

First, for the heading, Greece, you can use *grease*. From that, Link the pieces of information that you want to remember. For example, there's lots of *grease* on *a cross;* the cross jumps into the *sea* to *meditate* (across the Mediterranean Sea); then it swims away from a gigantic pyramid (Egypt) to a gigantic *pen* that's writing *unevenly* on a rock; it *coasts* over the pen; the pen has a *mane* like a lion and grease *lands* in it.

Review this. So far you've reminded yourself of: across the Mediterranean Sea from Egypt is a rocky peninsula with an uneven coast. This is the mainland of Greece.

See a lot of *yeast* (or eats) on the pen. The pen is growing a gigantic beard—it's *aging* (east of the peninsula, in the Aegean Sea). The gigantic beard breaks up into *lots of large and small* pieces that form *islands*. Lots of *grease* falls all over the place and starts living together and building *homes* (home of Greek civilization). A gigantic *nose* is also being built.

Nose, of course, is your basic Peg Word for 20. You'd probably be aware that you were reading about something that happened around 2000 B.C. and that you'd have to add two zeros to all the numbers. If you feel you don't want to take the chance, you can use *noises sue* or *nose sis*. You can also put something into the picture to remind you of B.C., although you'd know it couldn't be A.D. 2000!

See a gigantic *towel* (15: 1500 B.C.) covering the buildings and the nose. See people *writing* and *painting* on this gigantic towel. One of the paintings is of a great *palace;* see the writers and painters *fighting* most of the time. An *uncivilized tot* (11: 1100 B.C.) conquers the people who are fighting.

I've included all the facts in my Link, but usually, one *key* fact or picture will remind you of a number of facts. You should always include whatever you feel you need to remind you of the information. Go over the Link once or twice, and then try to fill in these blanks:

Across the . . . . from . . . . is a rocky . . . . with an . . . . coast. This is the . . . . of Greece. East of the . . . ., in the . . . . Sea, are lots of . . . ., some . . . . and some . . . . These lands were the home of . . . . tion.

The first Greeks probably came to the region about . . . . B.C. By . . . . B.C., some of them had a . . . . They knew how to . . . . and . . . ., and they built great . . . . .s. But they spent most of their time . . . . About . . . . B.C., they were . . . . by other Greek tribes who were not so . . . . .ed.

If you formed a good Link originally you should have breezed through this test. If not, go over the Link again and then try this:

In about what year did some Greeks have a civilization: . . . . B.C.

The Greek islands are in what sea? . . . .

Describe the mainland of Greece. . . . .

The first Greeks arrived in the area about . . . . B.C.

What country is across the Mediterranean Sea from Greece? . . . .

Besides writing and painting, the Greeks spent a lot of time doing what? . . . .

What happened about 1100 B.C.? . . . .

The Aegean Sea is (north, west, east, or south) of the peninsula? . . . .

Check your answers. You should have passed easily, even though I purposely mixed up the questions. It's important for you to realize that you knew the answers even though you originally memorized the material in sequence. Once you know the information, it doesn't matter; you can answer any questions, in any order.

The rhyming in most poems is a built-in memory aid, but you can remember a poem even if it doesn't rhyme. Read this short poem:

> The sun peeks out
>   with one purple eye.
> Without a blink
>   it searches the world,
>   noiselessly sighing
>   it sleeps again.

Easy enough. Start your Link with a picture of the sun peeking out over the horizon with one gigantic eye (the sun peeks out). If you want a reminder for "purple," put a Substitute Word or thought into the picture, perhaps a grape—a purple grape. Or see the gigantic eye being pulled, and it pays money *per pull* (with one purple eye).

The gigantic eye doesn't blink, no matter how many times it is pulled (without a blink). The sun holds a searchlight and searches all over (it searches the world). The searchlight sighs heavily, without a sound (noiselessly sighing), and lies down to sleep (it sleeps again).

If you want to memorize a quote word for word, apply the same idea. Here's one from Shakespeare's *As You Like It:*

> The whining schoolboy, with his satchel
> And shining morning face, creeping like snail
> Unwillingly to school.

You might picture a schoolboy whining, or if you like, he's drinking *wine;* see him carrying a satchel (or a *sad shell*), or drinking wine from a satchel. See a *face* on the satchel that shines so brightly it turns night into *morning.* Something that creeps like a snail shines brightly—or simply see a snail shining brightly. The last association of the Link might be a picture of a gigantic snail being dragged unwillingly into a school.

Try it. Use whatever Substitute Words or thoughts you like, of course. You'll be surprised at how quickly—and well—you'll memorize poems and quotes. The only way you can prove this to yourself is by trying it. Apply the system to any poem, whether or not it rhymes. The English language itself will act as a memory aid. If you remember the main thoughts or ideas, the ifs, ands, and buts will fall into place almost automatically. Apply the system as you would to any reading material; then go over it a few more times than you ordinarily would.

If you want to remember who wrote the poem, simply associate a Substitute Word for the author's name with the title. In the last example, see the schoolboy *shaking a spear* just the way *you like it.*

Practice the idea of remembering what you read, and no reading material will ever trouble you again—not so far as memorizing it is concerned. If you do it often enough you'll eventually be able to memorize facts while reading at your normal reading speed!

Also remember that the ridiculous pictures you form won't keep running through your mind (not that it can hurt you any). After you've used the information, once it becomes knowledge, they will fade.

Earlier in the chapter I mentioned headings. I'm sure you

understand the value of being able to Link chapter or section headings. A similar method is to read through something you'd like to learn, and underline the facts you want to remember as you come to them.

You know as well as I do that good reading is far more than merely recognizing words. Mechanical or passive reading must be changed to active, aggressive reading. Effective reading for study purposes would partly entail the art of boiling down hundreds or thousands of words to a few vital thoughts. Effective reading is a search—a search for ideas, thoughts, and answers.

Applying the systems you've learned will force you to read effectively because they will force you to locate the vital or key thoughts of any reading material. The search itself is a memory aid because you must concentrate as you do it. The thing to do is to lock in, or memorize, the vital facts or thoughts you locate. Then, after you have found and under-lined the facts, Link them!

Listening

Much of the material you must remember and learn you acquire by listening. There are courses that supposedly teach the student how to listen properly and effectively, but they all boil down to two words: pay attention. That is usually easier said than done.

Applying the memory systems to things you hear will force you to pay attention, and to maintain that attention. The main problem is that most people think much faster than they speak. There's a gap between the lecturer's rate of speaking and the listener's rate of thinking. It is during that gap that the listener's mind tends to wander. Once that happens, the student loses the lecturer's train of thought. When a student leaves a lecture thinking that he's forgotten most of what the lecturer said, what has really happened is that he never heard what the lecturer said in the first place.

Taking notes during a lecture is fine, except that, usually, while you're writing one fact the lecturer is discussing another, which you don't hear. How can you? You're too busy writing!

Applying the memory systems you've learned will force you to pay exclusive attention to the lecturer; there's neither time nor opportunity for daydreaming. You must listen for key words or thoughts, just as you search for them in reading material, in order to form Substitute Words and Link them. Just as with reading, you're turning passive listening into active and effective listening and learning. If you must take notes, all you need to write are the key words or thoughts. You can Link them after the lecture, if that's easier for you.

The important thing is that listening in order to hear the main points, which you must do in order to apply the memory systems, is like grabbing your mind by the scruff of the neck and forcing it to concentrate, forcing it to be Originally Aware! Even if the association idea didn't work at all, you'd still remember more of any lecture than you ever have before. Merely trying to apply the systems must better your memory for things you hear as well as for anything else.

Just to give you a goal to reach for: many of my students can listen to a lecture without taking a note and remember all the speaker's main points in sequence! The only way you'll start approaching that goal is to start applying the systems. Write some notes at first, just the key thoughts, and then link them. Each time you do that, you'll see that less note taking is necessary.

In the booklet I mentioned at the beginning of this book, teachers are advised to judge a student on how well he "is able to remember in sequential order facts taken from text." Teachers are also advised to judge the student on how well he "recalls main incidents in material read." On the same page it asks whether the student has developed "the ability to listen to a speaker and recall facts given." The memory systems are geared toward helping you do just those things!

38

LITERATURE

Remembering novels, plays, and poems and their authors is almost instantaneous when you apply the system. Form a good strong association between title and author, and one will remind you of the other. It will then be easier to remember than to forget them.

When studying literature, however, you will have to remember not only the title and author, but also the characters, plot, setting, and theme. Easy enough; your original association will be a bit more complicated, but then, you'll be memorizing more material.

Watch on the Rhine was written by Lillian Hellman. The main characters of the book are Kurt Mueller and Tek. The plot concerns a German refugee and a Nazi sympathizer meeting in an American home. The basic theme is good versus evil.

As usual, *you* must decide what to put into your association. Include the things that you feel you want to be reminded of. For example, you might see a *rhino* wearing a gigantic *watch* (*Watch on the Rhine*); a *lily*, dripping *Hellman's* Mayonnaise (Lillian Hellman—or *lily held* a *man*) comes out of the watch.

A mule (Mueller) hears the loud tick (Tek) of the watch and is curt (Kurt) to the rhino. You might see the mule wearing a swastika and the rhino trying to get away from it. The rhino runs toward an American flag, but the mule meets him there. That gives you the plot—a German refugee and a Nazi sympathizer meet in an American home. You can picture the rhino being very good and the mule being very evil; that will remind you of the basic theme. See these pictures clearly, and you'll remember the information you want to remember. (Do you see how valuable this idea is for book reports?)

A Tale of Two Cities by Charles Dickens. Main characters: Charles Darnay, Sidney Carton, Madame Defarge, Lucy Manette, Dr. Manette. The plot is the French Revolution and Carton's sacrifice (he dies in Darnay's place).

You might think this way: A gigantic tail has two cities on it; the inhabitants *quarrel* (Charles) like the "dickens." One of the quarrelers *darn*s on *A* (Charles Darnay) as he sits on a *carton* (Sidney Carton); an elegant lady (Madame) stirs *the fudge* (Defarge) that's in this carton; it's very *loose* (Lucy) fudge and a *man ate* (Manette) it all; the man that ate all the fudge needs a doctor (Dr. Manette).

You probably know the rest of it, but if you don't you can see all the fighters or quarrelers speaking with French accents (French Revolution) and picture the carton dying as the man darning an A walks away. You could also see the carton hitting a *sacrifice* bunt (baseball) so that the man on first, who is darning an *A*, can get to second.

You can remember concepts or philosophy the same way. A question that might be asked on a test is: "Upon what single principle is the philosophy of Epicurus based?" Answer: Epicurean philosophy is based upon the single principle of the infallibility of the senses. You might picture *a pea curin'* someone; it's doing it quite casually because it has complete confidence in the infallibility of its senses. It is saying, "My senses never fail; they are infallible." See this silly picture and you've memorized the question and the answer.

39

SHOW-OFF STUFF

I mentioned at the beginning of the book that you can use the Link and Peg methods to show off with. There are many stunts you can devise with the systems you've learned, and it is a good idea to show off with them because every time you do, you'll gain that much more confidence and ability. The more confidence and ability you have, the better you'll be able to apply the systems to your schoolwork.

You can demonstrate your great memory for letters and numbers by lettering a paper from *A* to *Z*, or from *A* to *M,* which is just as impressive and takes less time. Then tell a friend to call any letter and any two-digit number—in any order—and to write the numbers next to the letters.

When he's placed a two-digit number beside every letter, tell him to call any letter, and you will tell him the number. He can also call the number, and you will tell him the letter. You have to know the basic Peg Words and the alphabet Peg Words in order to do this demonstration, but if you know the words, it's easy. As the numbers and letters are called, simply make a good strong association between the letter word and the basic Peg Word.

Obviously, the better you know the Peg and alphabet words, the faster and better you'll be able to do this. End the demonstration just as you would a regular Peg list. Call off all the two-digit numbers from *A* to the end.

When you know the phonetic sounds really well, you can try the same thing with three-digit numbers. You'll have to make up a word or phrase for the number as soon as you hear it. For instance, for *L*-989, you can see an elevated train being puffed up—*puff* u*p,* 989; for *C*-914, visualize the sea full of *butter.*

You can also demonstrate your ability to remember long-digit numbers. With a bit of practice, you should be able to memorize a long number pretty quickly. Many of my students do it almost as fast as someone can write the number! Look at this: 6479470752948314707501.

A Link of shark (647) to bricks (9470) to clown (752) to perfume (9483) to trucks (1470) to closet (7501) gives you the number. Try it. A Link of only six pictures has enabled you to memorize a 22-digit number, forward and backward!

It doesn't matter how you break up the digits, and it's usually easier and faster to use *phrases*. A phrase is still only one picture in your mind. I've memorized the population of every state in the Union with this method.

An interesting stunt is to number a paper from perhaps 1 to 50. Without watching, have your friend call the numbers in any order and cross them out as he calls them. Tell him to stop when there are about five numbers left (not crossed out). Another way is to tell him to circle any five numbers first, and then to call and cross out all the others in any haphazard order. Then still without looking, you tell him which numbers he did not call!

How? It's easy, if you know the Peg Words from 1 to 50 *well.* As the numbers are called, you mentally *break or mutilate* the word or object that represents that number. That's all. Say 33 is called; see a mummy *coming apart.* If number 10 is called, picture a foot *without* toes. For number 12, picture a *crushed* can; for 36, a *broken* match. Just do that with every number (Peg Word) called.

When he stops, mentally go over your Peg Words from 1 to 50. Any Peg you come to that has *nothing wrong* with it is one of the uncalled numbers! Try it and see for yourself. When you come to a Peg Word that is not broken or mutilated, you'll know it immediately. This stunt is effective only if your friend crosses out the numbers quickly, and the only way to do it is to know the Peg Words well.

This is a good example of what I've been telling you—that the memory systems force you to concentrate on something, for a split second, as you never have before. The Peg Word makes the number meaningful, and mutilating the Peg Word forces you to concentrate on it for that split second. That's all that's necessary.

Anything you do to that Peg Word, mentally, will do. Instead of seeing it broken or mutilated, you can associate each one with yourself, or you can picture each one under water, or burning. It really doesn't matter. As long as you do something to each one, those you haven't done it to will stand out like a sore thumb. I use mutilation because it's faster.

There are many memory demonstrations you can do once you know the systems; I wanted to mention just these few. With a little bit of thought you can make up your own.

And, if you want to impress your parents or friends the next time you're sent to the store for some items, Link them. It's easy, and you'll never have to worry about losing a shopping list!

You can use the systems to remember anything, not only your schoolwork. You have to remember numbers and facts out of school, too; you might just as well make it easier and apply the systems. Let me remind you again that each time you do apply them, you'll be gaining confidence and ability.

40

LAST WORD

There's no reason now why you shouldn't be able to solve any memory problem. Understanding these systems is all that's necessary. There's always more than one way to attack and solve a problem; you only have to attack it in the way that solves it for you. When faced with a memory problem, think about it for a while. Then decide which idea, or ideas, can be applied in order to solve it, and apply those ideas. Of course, if you've merely *read* this book, go back and *do* the things that were suggested. Go back and practice; learn the fundamentals.

As with any mental or physical skill that you want to acquire during your lifetime, you will learn it only to the degree in which you master the foundation—in this case, the Link, Peg (phonetic alphabet), and Substitute Word systems.

Once you start to apply the systems to your studies and you see how well they work—how much easier they make studying, how much time they save you—you'll need no more prodding to make you learn and apply them. It's too bad I can't, in some way, show you the fascinating results of applying the systems. If I could, wild horses wouldn't keep you from learning them.

Of course, it is impossible to put everything about the systems in a book. There are some areas that cannot be explained in print. The only way for you to become aware of them is to use the systems yourself.

Only then will you see that the things that took me so many words to explain are almost instantaneous thoughts or pictures in your mind. Only then will you see what I mean by standards. The word "standard" means something you've used at least twice, so of course nothing can become a standard for you until you've applied the systems. And they can be applied to anything. Just remember that you are limited only by your own imagination!

Incidentally, with your knowledge of the Peg and Substitute Word systems, you can associate material in a book with its page number. One of my graduates was able to quote thirty-one law precedents and seventeen references (book title and page number) on a law exam. If you need Pegs for numbers over 100, simply make them up: 101—*test;* 134—*timer* or *tamer;* 212—I*ndian,* and so on. This idea can also be used as a fantastic memory demonstration, where you show that you've memorized an entire issue of a current magazine. If you associate the highlight of each page, such as pictures or advertisements, with the page number, you've really done just that.

The examples I've used have been general ones. Hopefully, some of them are things that you're studying now. It doesn't really matter. If you already know the material in some of the examples, you've still learned an idea that you can apply to other, similar material.

Some examples I've used may be material that you're not studying yet, but you may be studying it soon. Obviously, you should apply the ideas to the material you're studying now.

I've tried to use as wide a variety of examples as possible, but, even so, some may seem to be quite similar to others. There's no way to avoid that. I'd suggest you go over all the examples whether or not you think they're similar.

If applying the ideas seems just a bit difficult at first, keep at it. When you first learned how to skate, ride a bicycle, or drive a car, it seemed terribly difficult. Now you do these things without thinking. If you do think about them, it's probably to wonder why they ever seemed difficult.

The same thing is true of the memory systems. After a while, you'll apply them almost automatically. I've sold you no dreams in this book. The systems are definite. If you learn and apply them, you'll see results immediately.

Never lose sight of the most important aspect of the systems —the fact that they force concentration and awareness. They *must* do that if you try to apply them. That's why I've mentioned, a few times, that even if they don't work, they must work. By now, of course, you know that they do work.

It's also worth repeating that the ridiculous pictures you form will fade as you use the memorized material—as the information becomes knowledge. Don't worry about that at all. Also, don't worry about remembering too much; you'll *never* reach the full capacity of your memory. The more you remember, the more you can remember.

If you've used the systems, you've already bettered your memory to a great degree. You've also sharpened your concentration, observation, and imagination, and you've acquired a great sense of confidence. Just *knowing* that you can remember anything you want to usually makes it easier to remember it.

Therefore, the time you put into learning, practicing, and *using* these systems will be repaid many times over. It's like money in the bank; the more money you put in, the more interest you receive. If you don't apply the systems or learn the fundamentals, there will be no interest accrued. Remember, anything times zero is still zero!